A WARDER'S EXPERIENCES

IN

LANCASTER CASTLE

A WARDER'S EXPERIENCES IN LANCASTER CASTLE

BEING THE SUBSTANCE OF A PAPER READ IN THE LECTURE ROOM OF HIGH STREET SCHOOL, LANCASTER, BY THE LATE MR. ISAAC SMITH.

Late Sanitary Inspector to the Lancaster Corporation, and formerly a Warder in Lancaster Castle.

This version published in 2024
by Russell Holden & John Nixon

Page layout and cover design
© copyright Pixel Tweaks

ISBN: 978-1-913898-86-1

Book production by Russell Holden
www.pixeltweakspublications.com

Original publication printed and published
by Thos. Johnson, Church Street, Blackburn circa 1900

Foreword

by Bernard Wilson, retired prison governor

AN AMAZING POSTING

Earlier in my prison service career, when I was bag-carrier (Staff Officer) for the North Region Director of Prisons, I visited Lancaster Castle with him. While he was about his business with the Governor, I was fortunate enough to be given an insider's tour of the Castle by the Security PO. I was, dare I say it, captivated. The prospect of sometime myself being Governor was beyond my comprehension just then. When a couple of posting and promotions later I was in line for such a posting and a colleague 'phoned me to give me a list of vacancies with Lancaster among them, I can recall saying to him: "get off the phone, Frank, I need to make a call!" I immediately rang the Personnel Director's secretary and mercilessly lobbied her to speak for me to him…and it worked! My first in command post was Lancaster Castle. I can remember standing in my office looking out into that amazing place with such a great pride and amazing it proved to be. Being a Prison Governor is not an easy ride, but the place itself offered so many compensations and I can only give a flavour of them here.

THE AMBIANCE

I never during my term there felt anything but lightness of spirit, but stories of ghostly happenings and strange experiences abounded. It is a governor's duty to do regular night visits to his prison and I was no exception – and they could be entertaining at Lancaster. Some staff were quite reluctant to frequent certain areas, like the old execution yard, but it was ever on my itinerary. One Senior Officer who regularly rostered as Night Orderly Officer, seemed particularly susceptible to some feeling of discomfiture. One of the first jobs the Orderly Officer had to do was to go up to the radio room and turn over the set to "speak through" so that he could communicate to the Night Patrols whilst he was going about his own duties. I was advised that this officer always delegated this task to one of his team. My enquiries as to why found that on one occasion, he found himself on his way to the radio room in a small room at the end of a very old spiral stair, between two locked doors when his uniform jacket was grabbed quite violently from behind and he was dragged round – but to find he was very much alone! Hence his reluctance to retrace those steps on future occasions, but he didn't mind his junior colleague doing so. And this sort of experience was repeated in other locations at other times in some of the older places to some severe discomfiture among staff.

We were not over blessed with room and were needed to use all available accommodation. With this ever in mind, I was concerned to find that a certain cell on "the ones" on A Wing was being used as a catering store. I told the wing staff to get it cleared out and stuff relocated to the proper victualing store and the cell returned to normal accommodation. It didn't happen, so quite annoyed I enquired of the Wing PO what was going on. He took me aside in some embarrassment and advised me staff were disturbed because this cell was well known to be haunted. The last attempts to put a prisoner in there, they were faced with hammering on to the door from a very frightened man who swore the cell furniture – the bed with him in it- kept violently moving about. I said this was nonsense, but I was stubbornly resisted. I said that, OK make up the cell and I would come and sleep there to show it was rubbish. This was met over the next days with polite, but stubborn resistance. In the end, for the sake of staff harmony, I gave in and, to everyone's peace of mind, that cell was left to flour, salt et al and its poltergeist!

The reader may well enquire if I didn't wonder why, when left, comestibles were not liberally thrown around in that cell. Well, it did occur to me, but they weren't; such are the vagaries of ghost stories!

VISITORS

I welcomed any number of visitors during my time including Home Secretary, Douglas Hurd, Lord Montagu of Beaulieu among others. However, one time, perhaps associated with the paragraphs above, the Castle received a request for two members of the Coven Witches of America to visit, presumably because of the association of the Castle with the famous middle ages witch trials. The visit was agreed and two very unwitchlike young ladies visited and were given a tour of interest but apart from prisoner contacts. My Head of Works, Chief Officer Brian Oldroyd was delighted to do the honours and headed off with them having brought his camera with him to record the event. The two ladies, however, were quite reluctant to be included in his photographs. Brian, intrigued and not easily deterred, waited until their attention was diverted with the view from the top of the Keep and took a few sneaky shots just to have some record of the occasion. Sometime later, a rather shaken Works Officer came to see me with a roll of negatives and a story of a perfect set of negatives from before and after the event, but no trace of the frames he took of the two "witches". Photographers would, no doubt, have any number of reasons to explain the anomaly, but you may make of it what you will.

One far less spooky, but witch trial related occurrence happened on what must have been some anniversary, when a ladies' organisation from Pendle, the home of the famous so called witches, were doing, believe it or not, a sponsored "knit" making a knitted chain all the way from Pendle to the Castle and asked my permission for them to conclude right up to the Gate. I suggested they might like to go a stage further and finish their miles long line of knitting round the very iron ring set in the floor of the room where the poor creatures were manacled. That place was still there, unchanged after all those years down deep behind the Castle well behind an iron grill and a wooden door which, superstition says water, wood and iron together would ward off their evil spells. They were absolutely delighted and, accompanied by a TV camera crew, they did just that. Is that cell behind what was known for years as the Witches Well still there? I don't know, but I do know that that deep room has its origins in the earliest Roman remains.

ANTIQUITIES

There are many layers to the buildings and many odd bits that still remain, largely hidden and only hinted at that more knowledgeable folk than me can talk of-like the bits mentioned above that the ancient Romans left behind. One such is the old well head which is located somewhere under the clock tower. I had long been capped over when I was there, but I did have a conversation with an earlier Works Chief who recalled the well being capped. Before it was done, a sort of 'breaches boy' was set up and he was lowered down. He found the blocks constructing the walls of the well were wooden and when he had dropped quite a way down, he found a wide opening giving off to a passage, a passage that contained a Roman colonnade! That's not something I can verify and that particular individual is long gone.

FAMOUS TRIALS

There have been many famous and infamous trials like the witch trials, but in recent times, in fact in 1981 there was held the trial known as the handless corpse trial. It was before my time, but I do have a commemorative tie raised by the Police involved at the time. There has been much written to document those affairs; suffice to just mention it here.

Bernard Wilson

A Warder's Experience in Lancaster Castle

Prologue

In 1999, whilst emptying the house of a recently deceased Auntie, I came across an old and distressed-looking booklet titled *A Warders Experience in Lancaster Castle.* This booklet, written by a former prison warder about his time there in the 1860s, detailed his daily life, the conditions of the prison, and the experiences of the inmates. As a retired prison officer of over three decades, I had made several visits to

HMP Lancaster to transfer prisoners there over the years. So naturally, my interest was aroused by this old booklet. Whenever my duties took me to the Castle, I would always try to see as much as I could of the place whilst I was there and without fail, I would feel almost overwhelmed by its very long and, at times, bloody history.

My career began in 1974 at HMP Gartree Maximum Security Prison in Leicestershire, nearly a century after the events described in the Warder's Experience. This was a time of significant change in the UK, as capital punishment had been abolished less than a decade prior. Some of my colleagues had even carried out death cell duties.

I retired in 2006 from my last posting at HMP Haverigg in Cumbria, having witnessed many more changes in the prison system over the years.

A colleague at Haverigg, Mick Purvis, transferred to Lancaster Castle in the late 1990s and retired when the establishment ceased to be a prison in 2011. Moving to Lancaster Castle meant a significant change for him, and he was confronted with a completely different prison from the ones he had been stationed at previously. This was a medieval castle built on the top of a hill in the centre of Lancaster with a cobblestone road leading up to the gate, built on a small footprint, and built upwards, with most wings being five landings high. Despite the prison walls being some of the highest in Europe, a couple of escape attempts had been made with inmates trying to scale the walls. One pair managed to get to the top but underestimated the height and didn't have the means to get down the other side safely and ended up with broken bones.

Lancaster Castle has been a formidable fortress for centuries, and discovering the *Experiences of the Warder* in this found booklet – and a companion booklet '*The Gossiping Booklet, about Lancaster Castle* (discovered at a car boot sale) has given us an interesting insight into the everyday life of a warden and the inmates of this medieval establishment over a century ago.

John Nixon

Contents

Introduction

In the dimly lit corridors of history, haunting accounts echo through the stone walls of Lancaster Castle, reaching across the ages. This republishing of a personal account unveils the grim life within those formidable walls as witnessed by Issac Smith, a warder during the late 1800s. Locked within the annals of time, this narrative resurfaces to illuminate the shadows that once enveloped Lancaster Castle and its inhabitants.

We are transported back to an era when the echoes of clanging iron and the heavy sighs of the incarcerated permeated the air. The Wardens, custodians of justice and order, bore witness to the human drama unfolding within the castle's confines. Their pens, now long silent, captured the harsh realities of life, punishment, and redemption in an unforgiving era.

This republished account is a testament to the resilience of the human spirit in the face of adversity, offering a rare glimpse into the daily struggles, injustices, and fleeting moments of humanity within the cold and unforgiving stone walls of Lancaster Castle. where the echoes of history are preserved for future generations to contemplate and understand the trials faced by those who walked the corridors of this formidable fortress.

Join us on this journey through time as we resurrect the voices of Wardens and prisoners alike, allowing their stories to once again breathe life into the pages of this enduring narrative—a poignant reminder of the indomitable spirit that endured within the shadows of Lancaster Castle in the 1800s.

MR. ISAAC SMITH.

Late Sanitary Inspector to the Lancaster Corporation, and formerly a Warder in Lancaster Castle.

CHAPTER I

Introduction – Short History of the Castle – A Roman Fortress – A Baronial Residence – A County Gaol.

Who has not heard of Lancaster[1] Castle? Who has not started at the sound of a name so distinguished in history, so rife with associations at once romantic and painful! Many are the dark, cheerless stories told of this silent and mighty pile; many are the heartrending and frightful details which might be given of thee, thou last abode of crime and folly, and many are the prayers and curses heaped upon thy lofty head. Hundreds have, for the last time, bid adieu to friends, home, love, and all things connected with mortal state on first beholding thy weather-beaten towers!

It is admitted by all who have inquired into or written on the subject that Lancaster Castle is of Roman origin, a camp and fortress having been erected by Agricola about the middle of the first century. There is little reason, however, to suppose that any part of the original fabric remains.

1 Lancaster was recorded in the Domesday Book of 1086, as Lon-castre, where "Lon" refers to the River Lune and "castre" from the Old English cæster and Latin castrum for "fort" to the Roman fort that stood on the site.

Some historians have asserted that the father of Constantine the Great erected the square tower on the east side, adjoining the Governor's residence, and now called the Well Tower, about the year 305. This structure is remarkably strong, the walls being seven feet thick and apparently in as good preservation as they were on the day they were built.

From the period of the Conquest, when Roger de Poitou

enlarged the Castle and made his residence, down to the time of John o' Gaunt, nearly all historical details relative thereto are matter of conjecture. However, we have the best evidence for believing that John o' Gaunt 're-edified and endowed the Castle with all its original splendour,' whatever that might have been. He built the impressive Gateway Tower and made the Castle his residence, where he lived in princely state on the revenue of the duchy and the fortune of his wife, who was daughter and heiress of the first Duke of Lancaster. With his son, who ascended the throne under the title of

John o' Gaunt, Duke of Lancaster

CHAPTER I

Henry IV., the duchy of Lancaster merged into the Crown, and from that period the glory of the Castle and the town began to wane. The Castle ceased to be a baronial residence, and gradually sank from the proud position it had enjoyed as a place of entertainment for the highest and noblest in the land, until it ultimately became the receptacle for some of the lowest and most degraded, and such, no doubt, portions of the building are destined to remain.

It is true that the Castle in its entirety does not at present possess many of its former features, and those that remain give but a faint impression of its ancient grandeur; but it is nevertheless a noble edifice, and so far as regards its Roman and Norman portions, one of the grandest remains of antiquity of which this country can boast.

CHAPTER II

The Castle as a Debtors Prison – The Process of Whitewashing – Hansbrow's Castle Hotel – Life among the Debtors A Good Samaritan – Drink Smuggling and Smugglers –The New Bankruptcy Act.

I t was my lot to spend no inconsiderable my life inside this venerable pile, having been appointed an officer by the County Magistrates in 1861. At that time, the south side of the Castle was used as a Penitentiary for female delinquents, and the north side and Lungess Tower were appropriated to visitors who had come to undergo what was familiarly termed the 'process of whitewashing.'

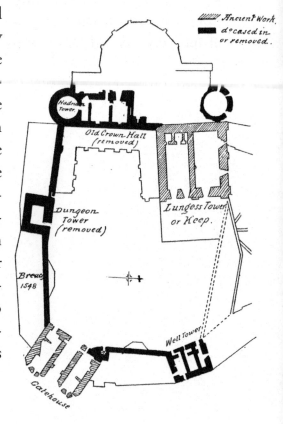

CHAPTER II

The friends and relatives of these latter people, who of course resided in various parts of the country, were wont to address their letters to 'Hansbrow's Hotel Hansbrow's Castle Hotel,' 'Hansbrow's Stone Just.' etc., Captain Hansbrow[2] being at that time Governor of the Castle. These gentlemen wore really insolvent debtors about ninety out of every hundred sent in by friendly creditors for the purpose of petitioning the Court to pay off their debts with a piece of waste paper. From 70 to 80 debtors went through this process every month. The whole affair was a huge swindle; only a very small percentage of the cases were genuine.

As a rule, a man went into trade and ran up debts to a few hundred pounds, paid as little as possible and put away as much loose cash as he could before his creditors became unduly pressing. When he found he could go no further he would persuade a friend to swear that he owed him over £20, and get him to take out a warrant and consign him to the Castle. I have frequently seen men waiting at the gateway of the Castle enquiring if the Sheriff's officer had not yet arrived with their warrant!!

---

2 Captain James Hansbrow served as the Governor of Lancaster Castle in the year 1852, overseeing the administration and security of this historic institution. His tenure marked a significant period in the castle's history, reflecting the societal and political dynamics of the Victorian era. Although specific details about his accomplishments or challenges during his governorship are not widely documented, the role played by individuals like Captain Hansbrow in maintaining order and justice within such institutions was crucial to the functioning of the legal and penal systems of the time. His service stands as a testament to the responsibilities and complexities faced by those tasked with the governance of institutions like Lancaster Castle in the mid-19th century.

There were several lawyers in the town who had offices in the Castle and employed assistants to bring them clients. The most important of these assistants was called the 'Cock-catcher.' It was his duty to meet the trains and bargain with the sheriff's officer to recommend his prisoner to his (the' Cock-catcher's') firm. This successfully accomplished the debtor was hurried into the Castle and into the presence of the 'Cock-catcher's' master, who after hearing the debtor story would tell him he could pull him through the Court for about £10, if he would sign a paper retaining him as his solicitor. Then the lawyer would draw up a schedule of ill his client's creditors with the amount of their claims, and a petition to the Court praying to be relieved from payment on the score of inability to pay. This done, notice was sent

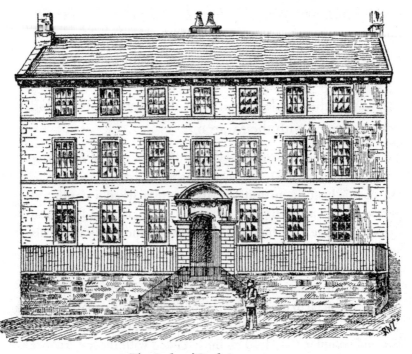

The Judges' Lodgings

to all creditors that if they intended to oppose the debtor's discharge they must give so many days' notice before the next Court day. If no notice was given the debtor was discharged as unopposed; but if the case was a bad one and a hostile creditor gave notice of opposing the petition, the debtor would get his friendly creditor to oppose likewise.

The hostile creditor would ask the judge to dismiss the debtor's petition for various reasons, while the friendly creditor would urge him to remand the debtor in prison for a few months, when they would perhaps be able to make better terms with him. The judge would most likely listen to the latter, and remand the debtor for perhaps six months at the suit of this creditor, who, like a good friend would forgive the debtor after the Court rose, and would lodge his discharge (which he probably had all the time in his pocket) with the Governor, with the result that the debtor would be discharged with the rest, the only drawback being that he could not obtain his certificate of discharge until the six months had expired. But with some debtors the wheel of fortune did not run quite so smoothly. Creditors were often obstinate. Suspecting that the debtor had the wherewithal to pay his debts, they would turn up on Court days in a body, and persistently oppose his discharge; and thus the game of 'tire you out' would proceed on both sides until one or the other gave way.

Though arrested under the same kind of writ, when inside the Castle the debtors were divided into two classes: the first class maintained themselves, but the second class lived at the expense of the county.

Lancaster Castle Courtyard

There were 22 rooms set apart for the use of the debtors-20 for males and two for females. Every debtor on entering the prison was charged a certain sum, termed 'room-money,' which covered the cost of fuel, lighting, the use of culinary utensils, &c., during the whole period of his incarceration, no matter how long. The money was collected by the 'rooms-men,' who had charge of the rooms, did the cooking, cleaning, &c., and waited upon the debtors in their respective apartments.

The fee varied with the accommodation from 25s[3], the highest sum, to 5s, the lowest. Subject to certain regulations any tradesman in the town had full liberty, at stated times of the day to convey eatables and drinkables into the Castle for the use of the debtors; and every morning a miniature

3 Equivilent to £457 in 2024

market, where butcher's meat, bread, butter groceries, vegetables, fish, and other commodities might be purchased was held in the Castle yard. Those among the richer debtors who did not care to purchase for themselves paid 78 or 88. weekly to the 'roomsmen' for their board, and this included a bottle of ale every day. Some of the roomsmen 'made a very good thing out of it; and money actually used to be made in the Castle by some of the debtors during their stay; even as much as £800, or bordering on that sum, is said to have been accumulated by one individual entirely from debtors, by advancing money to them at a most exorbitant rate of interest, on the security of watches, jewellery, and other articles which the borrowers were seldom able to redeem.

The best room was called the 'Quaker's.' It was a very large room in the Lungess Tower, being its full length and half the width. In my day this room was kept by old Ine Marsden, a man who went in as a debtor, and had 32 Christmas dinners in the Castle. He had the place furnished with easy chairs, sofas, a piano, and everything to make the room look comfortable.

There was a second-best room, where the board was not quite so high. This was kept by a man who had been six years in the Castle at the time of my appointment.

The first day after each Court-day the members of these rooms proceeded to elect a committee and officers to conduct the affairs of the room for another month. The officers were, Chairman, Vice-Chairman, Constable, Postman, and Cock-catcher. They had a code of rules printed and hung in the rooms, with a scale of fines for various offences.

The committee sat as a court once each month (or more frequently if necessary) to try the cases which it was the duty of the Constable to prefer. A debtor with 'the gift of the gab' would be told off to prosecute, and the offender could either defend himself or nominate someone to plead in his behalf. I have frequently witnessed great ability displayed at some of these mock trials, and not a little wit and good humoured banter is the examination of witnesses pro and con, as for instance

Counsel: You say that you know Mr Brown

Witness: Yes, Sir

Counsel: You swear that you know him?

Witness: Yes, Sir.

Counsel: You mean you are acquainted with him

Witness: Yes, Sir, acquainted with him.

Counsel: Oh, then you do not know him, you are only acquainted with him! Bear in mind that you are on oath, Sir. Now be careful. You don't mean to tell the jury that you know all about Mr. Brown, everything that he ever did?

Witness: No, I suppose

Counsel: Never mind what you suppose, please to answer my question. Do you or do you not know everything that Mr. Brown ever did?

Witness: No, I ...

Counsel: That will do, Sir. No, you do not to you are not aquainted with all his acts?

Witness: Of course

Counsel, Stop there, Sir, you are not called upon to make a speech, Are you or are you not acquainted with all his acts?

Witness: No.

Counsel: That is to say you are not so well acquainted with him as you thought you were?

Witness: Possibly not

Counsel: Just so, now we begin to understand each other. If you do not know anything about Mr. Brown's acts when you do not see him, you can't swear that you know him, can you?

Witness: Well, if you put it that way

Counsel: Come, Sir, don't seek to evade my question. I will put it to you again, When you say you know Mr. Brown you don't mean to insinuate that you know everything he does?

Witness: No, Sir, of course not

Counenl: Just so, of course not. Then you were not quite correct when you said that you know Mr Brown?

Witness: No, Sir

Counsel: In point of fact you don't know Mr. Brown.

Witness: No, Sir

Counsel: No, I thought so. That will do, Sir. You can stand down.

If a debtor chanced to come in with more money than brains he received the special attention of his fellows. He would be immediately nominated for the post of President, and, after a severe contest, elected. For this honour he must pay for the dinner beer for three days, and provide something special for Sunday's dinner. On the Monday following the Constable would summon the court and prefer some paltry charge against the President, the Vice' presiding. After an exhaustive trial he would be found guilty, fined, and expelled from the chair. A day or two after his friends would advise him to appeal for a fresh trial, which, of course, would be granted. His case would be re-heard, with the result that he would be acquitted, 'without a stain on his character,' and restored to his former dignified position, and made to stand beer again and a Sunday's dinner.

When a debtor was sent in by a hostile creditor this court would try his case if he chose, and advise him whether it would be wiser to face the judge or compound with his creditor. Here is a case in point: —A tradesman—a great swell—had been arrested in Liverpool under an absconding warrant, though I do not think he had intended to abscond. On arriving at the Castle he wanted to telegraph to his relatives and ask them to pay his debt; but his new friends of the Quaker's Room advised him to keep cool, and have his case tried by them. He ultimately assented, and they advised him to adopt the following plan, which he carried out with complete success: He wrote to his detaining creditor a very respectful letter, expressing regret at his inability to pay him in full, and as it would take all he possessed to see him through the Insolvent Debtors' Court, he thought it only fair (as he was his only creditor) to offer him the money instead of paying it away in law costs. He made an offer of 1s. 6d. in the £, which he said was the best he could do. Then he wrote a pathetic letter to his wife, telling her how he had got into trouble, that he had written to his detaining creditor offering all he had, which would only realise Is. 6d. in the £; that he thought his creditor was a humane, good sort of a man and would accept it; and telling her that in the event of his doing so she must sell the watch which her father gave her, also her jewellery and surplus clothing, and when he got out of prison he would try to make up for it all, even 'if he worked his fingers to the bone.' He then purposely made the mistake of putting his wife's letter into the envelope addressed to his creditor, and the creditor's letter into the envelope addressed to his wife, and posted them.

When the creditor opened the letter, which began "*My darling Wife,*" he was somewhat puzzled, but soon saw that a mistake had been made. In due time his wife sent the letter she had received on to the creditor, who naturally would say, Now I have by accident seen the real state of things; I may as well get what bit I can;' so he wrote accepting the offer of Is. 6d. in the & and sent the debtor his discharge. On leaving the Castle the discharged debtor gave £5 to his friends, with which to make merry over his success.

One other case. A Frenchman was brought in one night by two sheriff's officers. He had been speculating in mines, and his liabilities had run up to £120,000. He seemed terrified at the place, and would have given anything to be out. He wanted to telegraph to his solicitor to make an offer of 5s down 5s in six months, and 2s. 6d. in three months afterwards. However, it was too late to do anything that night, and his new friends urged him to keep cool and accept a little advice. He did so, with the result that within one week he was discharged on payment of 2s. 6d. in the £

One little incident will suffice to show how these gentlemen who usually live by their wits are determined to keep up the practice in whatever company they may find themselves. After one of the discharge days, when a lot of debtors had left the Castle, there remained in one ward three men; one was a notorious Manchester 'long firm' swindler, shrewd and intelligent; the second was a gentlemanly-looking man from London, with very agreeable manners, in fact very winning, both without money; the third was a merchant from Bradford, with good friends.

The three lived together, the two former manipulating the bills in such a manner that the latter had to pay nearly all the piper. But although he paid considerably over his share the others took care that he did not get above his share of the victuals. One Saturday they ordered duck and green peas for Sunday's dinner. It was early in the season for peas, so they were dear, and not only that, they did not shell out well. The two impecunious gentlemen thought there was not enough for three so they hit upon a plan to deprive of his share the man who paid for them.

One of the two reported himself sick, and obtained from the surgeon a couple of antibilious pills. Each of these he coated with a pea-skin, and at dinner was careful to put them upon the plate of his unsuspecting friend. 'Whist horrid taste exclaimed the two simultaneously, and when the Bradford victim got a pill between his teeth, he agreed that it was horrid enough, but when he got the second he gave up in despair and would have no more. The other two cleared the dish, but professed to do so under protest.

It ought to be mentioned that under the old Insolvent Debtors' Court system there was a Society in London called the 'Thatched House House Society,' who paid the lawyer's and court fees for such debtors AR could satisfy the Society that they were destitute.

While on this Good Samaritan part of my subject I will just record an incident which impressed me very much at the time, and made me wish that more would go and do likewise, A Mr. Ridley, of London, and friend, were visiting the neighbourhood of Lancaster, and, as was often the onse, had obtained permission to look over the Castle. I was appointed their guide. In passing through the gateway about half-a-dozen County Court debtors were brought in and marshalled in a row, whilst the officer examined their warrants.

Mr. Ridley asked me who and what they were, when I explained that they had been summoned by the County Court for debt, and not answering to the summons, judgment had gone against them by default, and they were ordered to pay what was probably just debt. The next court-day, as they had not responded to the order, the creditors had made application to the judge to commit them to prison.

In the whole of the cases it was found that an average of a little over £2 each would pay all. 'And should the money be paid down by a friend,' said Mr. Ridley, what would you do with these men?' 'We would simply open the door and let them go,' I replied.

Mr. Ridley took out his purse and paid the cash; and as some of the prisoners were forty or fifty miles from home, he also paid their railway fares.

Cases of delirium tremens[4] were very common, both among debtors and criminals. This was often caused through a prisoner having just had a heavy drinking bout, then being brought suddenly into the Castle, where he could not obtain another drop.

One very painful case was that of an actor from Barrow. He soon commenced to show symptoms of 'd.t.' and was consigned to the debtor's hospital. He spent a great part of the day in trying to pull down a heavy iron gate, his principal delusion being that someone was cutting his wife in pieces just outside. His appeals were most pitiful to hear. He would fall in his knees and pray to heaven for help in the most earnest language; then he would burl the hitterest curses at the heads of those who kept him from his wife. The poor Fellow got no better and was ultimately removed to the County Asylum, where he died a raving lunatic.

---

4 Delirium tremens (DT) is a severe and potentially life-threatening condition associated with alcohol withdrawal. It typically occurs in individuals with a history of chronic alcohol abuse who suddenly reduce or cease their alcohol intake. Delirium tremens is characterised by a combination of physical and psychological symptoms, including severe confusion, hallucinations, tremors, rapid heartbeat, high blood pressure, fever, and intense sweating.

CHAPTER II

Another case was that of a gardener from the neighbourhood of Garstang. He began to show symptoms after being in day or two, so he was removed to the hospital. The following night I was sleeping in the Castle, when the watchman awoke me, saying he thought there was a murder taking place in the hospital.

I at once got up and went to see, when an indescribable scene met my view. There were five other patients in the hospital, every one of whom was standing on his own bed armed one with a hrush-stick, another with a poker, and so on. The poor gardener was naked and mad, and rushing up and down the room as only a a madman could. When he came near one of the armed men he received a whack which certainly had not a soothing effect, and did not tend to improve my influence over him, for I had a desperate struggle before I could overpower him. It was a week before he got over the attack. These are specimens of scores of cases that might be recorded.

Though bottled ale might be purchased by the debtors to a limited exent, spirits were strictly forbidden; and tobacco, which at one time was allowed, became during the whole of my time, and for some time previous, contraband also. But many cute attempts were made to smuggle it in, some of which would occasionally succeed, but they were more frequently detected. On one occasion we had a debtor from Stockport a restaurant keeper, who catered for fifteen or twenty debtors in a small ward. His wife came over, to see him, when the turn key at the gate asked her the usual question before admitting her-

"Have you any tobacco or spirits with you?" "No," was the reply.

"I have reason to believe you have," said the turnkey, "and if you bring any in here you will be liable to fine or imprisonment. I will give you the chance of taking it away and leaving it somewhere till you come out." "I declare I have not a bit," she persisted.

"You had better be careful; you will be searched," continued the turnkey.

"Search away, I have none," was the reply,

A female warder was summoned and ordered to search, when it was found she had eight half-pounds of twist tobacco sewed carefully and equally round her crinoline. She was taken before the magistrates and fined £5, or in default a month's imprisonment

It occasionally happened that a debtor felt he could do with his overcoat, so he sent home for it. When it came it was found that it had been handed over to the tailor, who had taken out the padding and substituted tobacco, which he had nicely quilted over.

On one occasion a very handsome overcoat was piped all round with thin twist. A very common dodge was for a man to have a box of clothes or something else sent from home. A false bottom would be found in the box, and the cavity stuffed with tobacco. A man's wife or mother would be very good to him, and send him a box of groceries. Amongst the rest would be a Ilb, tin of mustard or coffee. On examination it would be found that the paper cover of the tin had been softened, the contents taken out, and the tin nearly filled with tobacco, a layer of mustard or coffee spread on the top, and the paper neatly replaced. Frequently tobacco (and occasionally spirits) would be found buried in the heart of a pie; and in various other ways did the friends of debtors endeavour to outwit the warders in their efforts to smuggle into the Castle these much coveted but strictly contraband luxuries.

A great change took place in Lancaster Castle, as in other similar places, when the Insolvent Debtors Act [5] gave way to a new Bankruptcy Act towards the close of 1861; but a greater change took place after the amendment of the Act, in 1868. After that year no one was supposed to be imprisoned for debt. At six o'clock on the morning of New Year's Day, 1869, the doors were thrown open, and all such prisoners shown the way out. There was still, however, a large number of debtors left in the Castle, who, it was stated, were not in for debt but for contempt of court-a few from the Court of Chancery, but the majority from the County Court.

---

5 Approximately 10,000 people were imprisoned for debt each year during the nineteenth century. However, a prison term did not alleviate a person's debt; typically, it was required that the creditor be repaid in-full before an inmate was released.The Debtors Act 1869 significantly reduced the ability of the courts to detain those in debt, although some provisions were retained. Debtors who had the means to repay their creditors but refused to do so could still be imprisoned, as could those who defaulted on payments to the court. Further reform followed through the Bankruptcy Act 1883. These acts initially reduced the number of debtors sentenced to prison, but by the early twentieth century, the annual number had risen to 11,427, an increase of nearly 2,000 from 1869.

Chancery Court debtors were committed during the pleasure of the Court, or until the contempt was purged: County Court debtors were sent for a stated period, varying from seven to forty days, and in some instances they were committed again and again for the same debt. A man from Bolton (if I remember correctly) was sent several times for forty days each time for one debt, which was originally only 1s. 6d.

We had two debtors in for contempt of the Court of Chancery eight or nine years; we had one in (a solicitor) about six years, who spent more money I should think every three months than would have paid the whole of his debts. The new Bankruptcy Act, however, turned him out, and, I fear, broke uis heart.

On one occasion there was a scene in front of the Castle gateway worthy of a place in the pages of Punch. As County Court debtors were sent from all courts in Lancashire, there were frequently twenty or thirty committed in one day.

One winter evening, between five and six o'clock, a very sudden change of weather set in, which caused the flags and paving- stones to be coated with ice. About twenty debtors were brought by train from various towns, and when they began to ascend the hill to gain entrance into Her Majesty's hospitable establishment, they began to slip and roll about like drunken men, and it ended in the lot of them crawling up on hands and knees to reach this haven of rest - a truly ludicrous spectacle.

CHAPTER III

The Crown Side of the Castle – The Chaplain on Drink
and Crime – Hard Labour – Shot Drill – Oakum Picking
Anecdotes of Irish Prisoners – Punishments – Dark Cell
The 'Cat' – The Birch – A' Poor Child' – Irish Grief.

For some years before the abolition of imprisonment for debt there were no male prisoners kept in the Castle, only prisoners awaiting trial. After trial those sentenced to penal servitude were sent to London, and short-time prisoners to Preston. After the debtors had cleared out a large corridor was built on the male side on the model gaol system, when we began to gain a little more experience of the criminal class. I am not now giving a temperance address, but I am bound to say here, most emphatically, that the experience we had would have been infinitely less but for the part played by intoxicating drink. I have by me an extract from the report of the Chaplain, presented to the Chairman and Justices at the recent Lancaster Quarter Sessions. It states that 'in the cases of 510 out of 577 men and boys under sentence in Lancaster Castle, either drink directly or drinking habits had led to the offences which brought the several prisoners under my notice. Against the names of 294 out of 388 female prisoners I had to write in my Character Book, the word 'drink.' Clearly, the man or woman who gets the least share of intoxicating liquor, gets the best share.

Every male criminal sentenced to hard labour, after passing the doctor, was put to shot drill for six hours a day and to oakum-picking for four hours.

Shot-drill consisted of a shot, or cannonball, about 26 lb. weight, being placed on successive blocks, about three inches from the ground and five paces apart. Every man stood with heels together facing his neighbour's back; at the word of command each man had to stoop simultaneously, with heels together and knees straight, pick up the shot, carry it in the hands level with but clear of the chest, step off all together left foot first, keep step, take five paces, close heels, and put down the shot on the next block, then rise slowly, knees straight, and repeat; time to rest, two

Shot-drill exercises

minutes out of every fifteen. I remember on one occasion being in command of this gallant regiment when they were inspected by his Majesty the Emperor of Brazil [Pedro II].

Shot-drill was a severe punishment to those unaccustomed to hard work; but to others oakum-picking was a greater, more especially if the oakum was a bad sample and the task a heavy one.

Oakum[6] picking is an art, and, like the crank or the treadmill, must be acquired by the slow and painful process of actual effort. It is the most irritating, evasive, minutely toilsome and painful work conceivable, especially to those who are not very handy with their fingers. An old hand thinks nothing of the full allowance, three pounds and a half, which he can pick, as the saying goes, 'on his head.' Unlike shot-drill and the crank, it requires no amount of bodily exertion,

---

6 **Oakum is a preparation of tarred fibre used to seal gaps. Its traditional applications were in shipbuilding, for packing the joints of timbers in wooden vessels and the deck planking of iron and steel ships; in plumbing, for sealing joints in cast iron pipe; and in log cabins for chinking. In ship caulking, it was forced into the seams using a hammer and a caulking iron, then sealed into place with hot pitch.**

Oakum was recycled from old tarry ropes and cordage, which were painstakingly unravelled and reduced to fibre, termed "picking". The task of picking and preparation was a common occupation in prisons and workhouses, where the young or the old and infirm were put to work picking oakum if they were unsuited for heavier labour.

The work was tedious, slow and taxing on the worker's thumbs and fingers. They had to pick 2 lb (910 g) per day unless sentenced to hard labour, in which case they had to pick between 3 and 6 lb (1.4 and 2.7 kg) of oakum per day.

Oakum picking

and consists merely of a pound or two of old rope, cut into convenient lengths, being picked into fine oakum in a given time; but I have frequently known cases of men, not used to prison life, doing their very best, up two hours before their time in the morning, and rubbing the skin off their fingers, being reported for not doing their full task, and sentenced to twenty-four hours' bread and water.

I recollect the case of an old Irish labourer from Preston, who had been making merry with his friends at his own house one Sunday afternoon, over the christening of his first grandchild. After tea the potency of the whisky began to tell, and the good fellowship ended in an Irish row, during which the old man stabbed his son-in-law, the child's father. For this he was committed to the assizes; and though his relatives did all they could to get him off-even to the son-in-law swearing that he ran against the knife the old man was sentenced to two years' hard labour. He was too clumsy for prison life-awkward at shot-drill, not able to do his task at oakum-picking and being very untidy in his cell he was continually in trouble, reported nearly every day, and every time reported he was put upon bread and water for the usual number of hours. I felt really sorry for the old man, and when an opportunity occurred for re-arranging prisoners, I contrived to have him removed into a cell under my charge, so that I could help him a little. One day, after having been with me a few months, he was visited by a Roman Catholic priest from Preston while I was at dinner. When I returned I went into his cell and found him on his knees with his prayer-book opened (but still working away at his oakum-picking) and sobbing and crying bitterly.

"Come, come." said I, "If the priest's visits upset you like this, we cannot allow you to see him again."

"Oh, it isn"t that. Mr. Smith; I was thinking of my friends at home," he replied.

"Well," I said, "you know if you were set at liberty tomorrow you would be back here in a week. You would drink with the first man that asked you to have a glass of whisky if you had the chance,"

"No, never no more; not another drop," he replied. "Why. Mr. Smith, I was teetotal for two years."

"Then why did you not remain so?" I asked.

"Well," said he, "I will tell you. I was working at Bolton, and I was paying my club-money at a public-house when a 3d. check was given me for drink. I had given away my check and was going out when I met a friend who said, 'Hugh, come and have a drink'. 'No, thank you,' said I, 'I'm teetotal.' 'Why, man, I can see you are,' he said, 'you're dying;' and he persuaded me";

And bursting into a flood of tears and lifting up his eyes to the roof of his cell, with his hands clasped, he exclaimed, "Look, Mr. Smith, I wish, I wish, my heavenly Father had put it into my head to punch the b—down stairs and break his b—neck!"

Here is another little incident, the recollection of which sometimes makes me smile. One morning, on escorting the Governor round on his daily visit, I threw open the door of a cell in which was confined an Irish vagrant. Now, this man, as in all cases, was instructed to keep his cell scrupulously clean, his blankets neatly folded, and when the Governor entered his cell he was to stand at attention and salute him. But he did none of these acts of discipline; and as the Governor (Captain Hansbrow) looked round the cell he found fault first with one thing and then another, and finally threatened him, in his somewhat eccentric manner, thus:

"Now look here, sir, this won't do; this won't do; if I have to speak to you again I must punish you; I'll be down your throat, sir; I'll be down your throat!"

As he repeated this threat several times, I saw a twinkle come into the man's eye, and after the last threat of 'I'll be down your throat,' he exclaimed,

"Begorra, Sor, I wish you or something else was down my throat, for my back an' my belly's stickin' together!"

26

CHAPTER III

When a prisoner gets the first half of his time over he begins to be hopeful, and counts the weeks, days, hours, and often minutes that shall set him free. About a week or so before a prisoner's time expires, by asking the Governor, he is permitted to write to his friends for money to pay his expenses home, for for other necessaries. On one such occasion a prisoner asked this permission: 'How long have you to stay yet?' enquired the Governor. 'Please, Sir,' was the reply. 'Ive a fortnight and two days the day but one after to-morrow.'

The most severe form of punishment in the power of the Governor for breach of prison discipline was to order the refractory⁷ prisoner to be locked up in a dark cell for three

---

7 **Refractory: one resisting control or authority : stubborn, un-manageable: resistant to treatment or cure**

Refractory eh? Bread and water for three days and the use of the dark cell.

days and nights without bed, his diet being six ounces of bread three times a day with a drink of cold water. For any more severe form of punishment the prisoner had to be taken before a visiting magistrate.

We had a youth who was a very sullen, stupid-tempered fellow. On one occasion he quarrelled with his food, and took neither bite nor sup for nearly five days. A second time he tried it, and reached the ninth day, when it was decided to force food into him, but he came round. Soon after this, for an assault on one of the officers, he was taken before the magistrates and sentenced to one month's solitary confinement, and 24 lashes with the cat.' That is the instrument for breaking a man's spirit! It is a long-handled nine-thonged whip, the lashes of which are made of very hard cord about one-sixteenth of an inch in diameter, with knots four inches apart.

When this is used the victim is stretched out so that he cannot move a limb. His feet and legs are strapped tightly to the two front legs of the triangle, and in the apex there is a pulley to which two leather handcuffs are attached. These are put round the wrists, and the hands are drawn up till the arms are at full stretch.

CHAPTER III

The first few strokes usually draw blood, or, rather, cut right into the flesh, and only the strongest and most callous can stand the full number of 36 lashes without fainting. Of course the doctor stands facing the victim, and can stop the punishment at any moment.

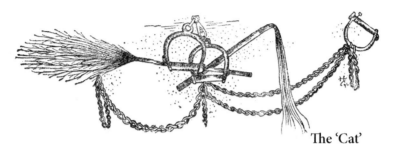

The 'Cat'

To see a man flogged is a sickening and degrading spectacle. I was never called upon to use that instrument of torture called the 'Cat,' and if I had been I do not think I should have carried off a prize as a first-class performer. A similar kind of punishment occurred much more frequently, and was to me equally repugnant: that was in the case of boys sentenced by the magistrates to a dozen or two dozen strokes with the birch-rod. This was no light punishment when it is remembered that the first stroke would raise weals on the back the eighth of an inch; I will leave it to the imagination what a dozen or so more strokes on the top of that would feel like.

This duty was supposed to be discharged by each officer in turn, and the Governor and doctor were required to be present and witness the punishment. I, however, contrived to get out of it on every occasion but one, and that was in the case of a lad from Skerton, who was perhaps the worst juvenile offender we ever had in the Castle. I managed to get through the performance in a fashion which elicited a left-handed compliment from the Governor, who, with a cynical smile, exclaimed, "Do you call that flogging?" The boy, to show his gratitude to me and his contempt for the Governor, as the latter turned his back, put his thumb to his nose and said to me with a wink, "I don't care now it's over!"

One day a man from Barrow was brought in for a month, on a charge of being drunk and riotous. He had several times previously visited us, and had always been very troublesome to the doctor. He was a Welshman, over six feet high and weighed about 16 stones. On this occasion, towards night, as the drink was dead in him and he was a bit shakey, he felt very anxious to see the doctor. He was evidently suffering from a touch of bronchitis so I made him a good hot mustard poultice, which made him howl and dance round the place like a bear with a sore head. He still demanded to see the doctor, and on my remonstrating with him he began to cry, and said, 'Oh, have pity, Mr. Smith, and remember that I am some poor mother's child !'

I once witnessed a very harrowing scene at the close of the assizes. Four young Irishmen (two married and two single) had come over from their own country and got a job at some public works in the neighbourhood of Accrington. They had hoped, so they said, to save a little money to take back to Ireland, with which to 'pay the rint;' but one Saturday night they adjourned to a public-house, and after spending an hour or two there in imbibing a big dhrop of the craytur[8],' they

---

8 whiskey (Irish, slang). 'A drop of the craytur'. This is the origin of the modern term "creature comfort"

An execution on modern principles

became very quarrelsome with the rest of the company. A fight ensued, when one of the Irishmen ran into an adjoining cottage, and seizing a poker rushed out with it and stuck it into the eye of one of the combatants, death being the result. All the four were sentenced to penal servitude for life. Parents, wives, and sisters came over from Ireland, and after the trial were permitted to have an interview with the prisoners before they returned. That interview baffles description. Contrary to custom (because time was short) they were all allowed to have the interview together. A table was placed in the room between the prisoners and the visitors; but in a very few minutes the table was useless, for there was presently an outburst of wild Irishism such as I never before nor since witnessed. The table was overturned,

Condemned

and visitors and prisoners fell upon one another with every manifestation of real Irish grief crying, yelling, howling, hugging and kissing-a scene unparalleled within the walls of the Castle. They were with great difficulty separated, when the prisoners returned to heir separate cells and the friends to their homes. What a terrible price to pay, thought I, for a glass or two of whisky!

Among the peculiarities observable may be mentioned the monotonous ring of the Castle bell. This bell was rung on ordinary occasions three times a day, viz., at six in the morning and seven and nine in the evening. Hanging in the gateway, it was usually rung by the turnkey who had charge of the gate, and so singularly melancholy and startling was the sound, that in some prisoners it produced an indescribable sensation on first hearing it. It was something between a ring and a toll, after this manner (pronouncing each o long and deep, as in and pausing at the end of each line):- 'toll,'

Tolly-toll-loll; Tolly-toll-loll;

Tolly-toll-loll;

Toll!

It is recorded that a prisoner was brought into the Castle in very low spirits, and that on the first stroke of the bell he leaped from his seat in the most frantic manner, and was taken out a lunatic, complaining that he perpetually heard the bell ringing.

This bell is also used for the last solemn duty of announcing to the public the departure of all unfortunate creatures condemned to death. It has sounded the death-knell of 228 human beings[9].

---

9 Before 1834, there were as many as 20 offenses, not limited to murder, that often led to execution. Out of the hangings recorded between 1800 and 1865, only 43 (20 percent) were for murder. Burglary, highway robbery, uttering (passing forged bank notes), arson, and theft of sheep and horses accounted for the rest.
Saturday was the customary execution day at Lancaster, likely chosen to maximise deterrence by ensuring a sizable audience. The highest mass hanging occurred in September 1801 with eight simultaneous executions. Ten more executions took place that year. The peak year for hangings was 1817, witnessing a total of 20 executions.

Crown Court, Interior

CHAPTER IV

The Hanging Town – Weeping Hill – Sentenced to Death
Suicides – Refractory Prisoners – Forbidden Communications
Visitors to the Gaol – Their Generosity and Appreciation
Professor Owen and the Negro's Head.

Before assizes were held at Liverpool and Manchester, Lancaster was known in South Lancashire as the 'hanging town.' In *The Gossiping Booklet about Lancaster Castle* we have full and accurate details relative to the most gruesome subject of public executions at Lancaster from the beginning of the nineteenth century down to the passing of the Private Executions Act in 1868 (see page 51). There is, however, an omission in that deeply interesting booklet which I will supply here, in as much as the circumstance I am about to relate is very little known among the younger generation of Lancastrians.

When, as I have just said, Lancaster was the 'hanging town' for the whole county, prisoners for trial were brought from the southern and eastern portions of Lancashire in coaches and other conveyances, heavily manacled. As they entered the town from Scotforth there was a most noble and beautiful view of the Castle and Church, now much marred by the numerous residences which have sprung up in recent years.

The spot was known as 'Weeping Hill,' because from this point the great prison of the county could be seen in all its terrible majesty, as it burst suddenly in view of those who were travelling to its gates, and often to their certain place of doom. Readers of Wordsworth's poetry will perhaps call to mind the following 'Sonnet, suggested by the view of Lancaster Castle on the road from the south'-

> *This spot at once unfolding sight so fair*
> *Of sea and land, with yon grey towers that still*
> *Rise up as if to lord it over air-*
> *Might soothe in human breasts the sense of ill,*
> *Or charm it out of memory, yen, might fill*
> *The heart with joy and gratitude to God*
> *For all his bounties upon man bestowed:*
> *Why bears it then the name of 'Weeping Hill?'*
> *Thousands, as towards yon old Lancastrian towers,*
> *A prison's crown, along this way they past*
> *For lingering durance or quick death with shame,*
> *From this bare eminence thereon have cast*
> *Their first look-blinded as tears fell in showers*
> *Shed on their chains; and hence that doleful name.*

I do not intend to dwell at great length upon this part of my subject: it is too awful. It has frequently been my duty to watch both day and night by the side of criminals sentenced to death. Some cases were most distressing; but in others I may say there was a certain amount of edification.

CHAPTER IV

One very very touching case was that of a mechanic from the north of Ireland, whose parents were members of a Presbyterian Church. While with them he had promised well; but he left the parental roof and went to Barrow, where trade was good and wages better than at home. While there he unfortunately made companions of those who spent their evenings in the public-house. One Saturday night not knowing what he was doing, through being maddened with drink-he stabbed to death a man upon whom he looked when sober as his best friend. For this he was condemned to death; and his was the first private execution within the walls of the Castle. He was an intelligent young man, and had received a good religious training.

His remorse and repentance were, I firmly believe, very deep and sincere. He never complained of his own punishment, his grief was in the contemplation of the sudden and untimely end of his friend, and the dark cloud he had brought over his relatives at home. But the Word of God became the power of God for his salvation. We frequently read together suitable passages of Scripture, and unitedly supplicated the Throne of Grace, until presently the rays of the Son of Righteousness penetrated his heart, and he began to realise that though his crime was great, the blood of Christ could cleanse from all sin; so that eventually that peace 'which passeth all understanding' entered into his breast; and though he died the death of a felon, I believe the angels were waiting to usher him into the presence of his Redeemer.

Another case, much different from the above, was that of young man from Preston, about 21 years of age, married, with two children, his wife being two years his junior. He was put of work, and as he, with a companion and a dog, was walking down the street his dog flew at a cat sitting at a cottage door. The owner of the cat (an old woman) struck the dog with a broomstick, which so enraged the owner of the dog that he kicked the old woman, pushed her down a few steps and broke her leg. He was committed for an assault, but afterwards, as the old woman died, he was re-committed for manslaughter. After reading over the depositions before the trial, the Judge directed the grand jury to bring in a bill for wilful murder. with the result that he was tried, found guilty and sentenced to death.

He was a poor, soft, ignorant lad, who expected about 12 months' imprisonment. When sentenced to death he was completely staggered. I was with him in the dock, took him to the condemned cell and remained with him all night. But never before nor since have I spent such a night! He professed to be a Roman Catholic; but I do not think he was of any religious denomination, in fact, he could not tell me who Jesus Christ was.

I did my best to comfort him by reading suitable portions of Scripture; and now and again he would look up and say, "Ay, Maister, why couldn't somebody tell me that afore?" I should think that hundreds of times, after giving him some comforting message, he would jump out of his bed on to his knees and kiss my hand.

After ten days or a fortnight his sentence was commuted to penal servitude for life; and though that was bad enough, yet to witness the joy that filled his soul when the Sheriff came to tell him that Her Majesty had been pleased to spare his life, was enough to thrill one with equal delight. "Oh," he said, "so long as they don't hang me, I don't care what they do with me."

I might refer to several other similar cases, but I will briefly mention one of a different type from the foregoing. An old man (a respectable tradesman) after a wasted life turned up in his native place, and a former chum, in fairly good circumstances, took him into his house. Eventually the chum died from poison, and the man was charged with having caused his death, the supposed motive being that if he could get his chum removed and could marry his widow, he might then live in the same comfortable circumstances as his whilom friend. He was tried on the capital charge, found guilty and sentenced to death, but for some reason his sentence was commuted to penal servitude for life.

During his incarceration he manifested the most rancorous spirit; charged Governor, Chaplain, and officers with being in league against him, and if any little act of kindness was offered him he repelled it in the most insulting manner. When his respite arrived he said the authorities were too cowardly to hang him, and used the most filthy language.

No one was sorry when he left the Castle.

It has been my painful duty on several occasions to cut down prisoners who have attempted suicide by hanging, and once when a prisoner had carried out the deed. One Saturday, during the assizes, an old farmer was found guilty of the manslaughter of his wife and sentenced to penal servitude for the remainder of his life. I took him his breakfast at 8 o'clock on Sunday morning; two hours afterwards I accompanied the doctor on his usual morning visit to the cells, when we were horrified to find that the prisoner had fixed his pocket handkerchief to a low cupboard in the corner of his cell, tied his neckerchief, which was round his neck, to that, laid down on the floor and so strangled himself.

A word or two with reference to refractory prisoners. I do not think we should have had any on the male side if, as it sometimes a prisoner had not imagined that he was Prest unfair treatment. A man would be put upon bread and water again and again for minor offences, or for not doing his work satisfactorily; but he rarely kicked up a row, or refused point blank to do his allotted task. But with the women it was different. The monotony of prison life was more irksome to them; so on the slightest pretext they would break out—perhaps smash the windows or tear up their clothing.

A male officer was generally sent for to lock them up in the 'refractory cell,' which meant no bed, and bread and water for three days and three nights. But to secure them in the first instance sometimes required no little strategy, for they would arm themselves with a formidable weapon in the shape of a rubbing-stone placed in the foot of a stocking, which they would swing round with more or less violence the nearer you approached them, or kept at bay.

Prisoners were frequently punished for trying to communicate with each other. This they sometimes attempt by putting the mouth close to the hot water pipes, by means of which the sound was transmitted to the next cell. As the officer went round occasionally and could look through a small spy-hole into each cell without the occupant's knowledge, the prisoner who was caught indulging in this little luxury was made to pay for it.

One of the most common methods of communication was practised in the chapel during service, which was held once every week-day and twice every Sunday. We once had in a regular old jail-bird, awaiting trial for burglary. It was a few days before the assizes, and, as was the rule, there had been brought into the Castle all the prisoners awaiting trial at Preston, so the prisoners had to sit in chapel a little closer than usual.

As the man was known to be full of mischief he was placed in a corner, and an old farmer, who was charged with the manslaughter of his brother, was placed next to him. From what I saw and afterwards learnt from the old farmer, something like the following took place: When the Chaplain led off, 'Our Father,' &c., the jail-bird looked me straight in the face, and, as though he were following the Chaplain, he asked the old man (intoning all the time) What's thy name?' Where does ta come from? What has ta been doing?' As the old man knew he was liable to punishment if caught talking, he held his tongue, but the other continued and threatened what he would do if he did not answer. But the old man was firm; so when they were sitting down the jailbird contrived to get his hand under the old man's leg and inflicted a severe pinch, and again whe when intoning said, 'If tha doesn't answer I'll What's off' pull thy leg What's thy name? ta sent here for?' The old man at length replied, 'My name is so and so, and they've sent me for killing my brother.' Then they'll hang thee, tha old b,' was the intoned reply.

I will just relate an incident or two relative to persons visiting the Castle. Hundreds of visitors came daily in summer; but as a rule they were only permitted to see the court-yard, dungeon, and law courts. Parties able to obtain a magistrate's order were allowed to see portions of une inner working of the prison; and this privilege is nearly always accorded to gentlemen serving on the jury at Quarter Sessions and Assizes, by order of the Chairman or the Judge.

The first place visited is usually the dungeon, under the Well Tower-the oldest part of the Castle. This being one

of the show places which every body sees, there is no need
to describe the damp walls, the iron rings in the floor to
which the Pendle witches[10] were chained, or the arched and
vaulted roof which has so well withstood the ravages of a
thousand years.

> ### THE
> # WONDERFVLL
> ## DISCOVERIE OF
> ### WITCHES IN THE COVN-
> ##### TIE OF LAN-
> ##### CASTER.
> ### With the Arraignement and Triall of
> Nineteene notorious WITCHES, at the Assizes and
> generall Gaole deliuerie, holden at the Castle of
> LANCASTER, *vpon* ᴄMunday, *the se-*
> *uenteenth of August last,*
> 1 6 1 2.

Modern jerry-builders might derive a useful lesson therefrom,
but every-day folk usually find great relief on emerging from
this Stygian cave into the open daylight of the court-yard.
The lofty rooms in the Gateway Tower, said to have been
the state rooms of John o' Gaunt and other notabilities,
are also shown.

---

10 **The trials of the Pendle witches in 1612 are among the most
famous witch trials in English history, and some of the best recorded of the 17th century. The twelve accused lived in the area
surrounding Pendle Hill in Lancashire, and were charged with
the murders of ten people by the use of witchcraft. All but two
were tried at Lancaster Assizes on 18–19 August 1612, along with
the Samlesbury witches and others, in a series of trials that have
become known as the Lancashire witch trials. Of the eleven who
went to trial – nine women and two men – ten were found guilty
and executed by hanging; one was found not guilty.**

It is needless to say they are not now used, though the Constable of the Castle-an honorary office, held at present by the Right Hon. Sir J. T. Hibbert-had the right to use these 'state' rooms for a certain period each year as his official residence. The owl and the jackdaw, however, appear to have supplanted him. A visit to the leads on the top of the Gateway Tower reveals the primitive and barbaric yet efficacious method of ancient warfare. Heaps of stones are piled in a small building, which also contained the appliances for melting lead and other metals. The stones and molten lead could be dropped upon the heads of an attacking force through the spaces in the masonry left for that purpose, whilst the defenders were completely protected behind the solid battlements. Here too can be seen the remains of the old spike on which were stuck the heads of traitors and others, as a warning to the people outside.

Crossing the court-yard-with the Penitentiary, bearing the figure of Justice, blindfolded and holding the even-balanced scales in her hand, sculptured on its front, on the left the visitor is shown into the Chapel, a bright and cheerful-looking place, separated along its whole length by a high screen, which divides the men from the women. Texts and exhortations are profusely displayed, and these may sometimes be the means of fixing gospel truths in the minds of the prisoners. It is easy to imagine that the service hour will provide a welcome break in the dull monotony of prisoners' lives, whether they profit by the ministrations of the Chaplain or not. In a recess to the right of the pulpit and just within the door, is the seat occupied by a condemned prisoner during the days that intervene between the trial and execution, whilst in the gallery a few seats are screened off from the others for the use of juvenile offenders.

Bird's-eye view of Lungess Tower and Shire Hall

The scaffold the dread instrument of the law, which still demands 'a life for a life'-used to be erected in the chapel-yard since public executions were abolished, and the sombre and circumscribed surroundings were in strict keeping with the tragedies enacted under legal sanction. The chapel steps are no longer used as the ascent to the platform from which the fatal drop is taken, for a new and much more up-to-date scaffold has been constructed near the wall opposite the church- yard, not far from the spot where so many criminals have been hung when outside executions prevailed. The new scaffold is constructed on the ground level, so that there are no steps to climb, and the 'pit' is a permanent cellar underneath the drop. The gallows is constructed to receive three culprits at once, and the 'drop,' worked by the executioner by means of a lever, is similar in construction to the one connected with the old scaffold.

In the office, which is also shown, is a model of the old scaffold, and the book in which the list of executions kept, as well as the crimes that led to the last terrible sentence of the law being carried out. It contains some startling entries.

Crimes that are now frequently punished with a few months' imprisonment were in the old days visited with death by hanging, and such a record as this proves that the law and those who administer it are more merciful than in the 'good old times.'

The Law Courts, Adrian's Tower with its Roman antiquities and other curios, the Drop-room, Lungess Tower or Keep are also shown.

On one occasion I was sent for to escort round a clergyman from Devonshire and his wife. They were an elderly couple, very nice, fond of antiquesties, and were greatly interested in the place. The lady was anxious to get to the top of the Keep, but seemed afraid of the dark winding staircase leading thereto. She got over that difficulty, however, and reached the summit, only to find the descent so much worse than the ascent that I had to take her in my arms and carry her to the bottom. They were both rapturous in their appreciation of their visit, and on leaving the gentleman said, 'I am sorry to see there is a notice on the door forbidding me to give you anything for your kindness, and as a clergyman I should be very loth to break your rules; so I will not give you anything, but when you have locked the door of the court look round the corner and see if you can find anything; I did so, and found half-a-crown. A similar incident occurred shortly after, when a party of Quakers[11], who were particularly anxious to see the room in which George Fox was confined, were being shown round. On finishing their tour the leader of the party offered his thanks, and said he would have been pleased to give something but found it was against the rules, so he said, 'I'll tell thee what I'll do: I'll lend thee half-a-crown, and I'll never ask thee for it back.'

---

11 Among the Quakers incarcerated in the Castle, a select few underwent trials, with notable proceedings involving Margaret Fell and George Fox. Margaret Fell, during her 1664 trial, declined to take the oath, voiced grievances about the prison conditions, and engaged in disputes with the judge. Following a subsequent trial, she received a four-year imprisonment sentence within the Castle.

Similarly, George Fox faced clashed with the judge due to his refusal to remove his hat. In the seventeenth century, the practice of "hat honour," involving the removal of hats in the presence of social superiors, was customary. However, Quakers, adhering to their belief in the equality of all people before God, abstained from this custom. Fox managed to persuade some justices to visit his place of confinement, describing the deplorable conditions, including rain, wind, a deteriorating floor, and others characterising it as a rudimentary toilet.

The adverse prison conditions led to the deterioration of health and even death among numerous Quaker prisoners, with thirteen recorded deaths in the Castle. Causes of death ranged from diseases and injuries to violent arrests or the exacerbation of existing illnesses due to the prison environment. The last documented death of a Quaker prisoner within the Castle occurred in 1720. In the early eighteenth century, several Friends remained incarcerated for their refusal to pay tithes.

I will conclude these rambling reminiscences with an anecdote for the truth of which I cannot vouch, as the circumstances took place long before my time. It is well known that the late Sir Richard Owen, the eminent anatomist, was a native of Lancaster, and was born in Dalton Square, 20th July, 1804.

After quitting the Grammar School he became a pupil of Dr. Baxendale, then a prominent medical practitioner in Lancaster and surgeon to the Castle.

It was usual at that time to hand over the bodies of malefactors after execution to the surgeons for dissection; but young Owen had a horror of the ghastly details of the business, which he imagined he could never overcome. He was cured, strange to say, by a fright.

Having to take some medicine on a windy night to the Castle, he had to pass through the room in which he had taken part in dissections. Just as he entered the room with the basket of medicine under his arm, the clouds which hid the moon suddenly parted, a door slammed, and, looking up, the future biologist saw what he thought was an enormous figure in white, with outstretched arms, looking down upon him. He dropped his basket and ran. But when he returned next day and found that he had been frightened by mortuary sheets, he braced his nerves up so that he was soon collecting skulls. He made a fine

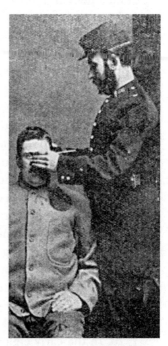

Taking measurements for future identification

set, but for a long time he could not get an Ethiopian skull.

At length a negro died in the Castle, and the young doctor got permission to add his head to the collection. It was again a stormy night when the operation of removing the head was determined upon. But habited in his long cloak, then the fashion, and provided with a blue bag, the comparative anatomist soon had the head carefully stowed away. As he left the room in which the headless corpse lay, however, the wind slammed the door violently, caught his cloak, and nearly threw him upon his face.

Attempting to recover himself, he lost his hold of the bag, the head fell out, rolled with increasing velocity down a flight of steps, and settled itself upon the neck in a room where two women shrieked.

The professor rushed wildly after it, took no notice of the women, seized the head, put it in his bag, and made the best of his way out.

Four or five years afterwards he was attending a dying woman, who called loudly for a clergyman, to whom she had something to tell. The doctor begged her to tell him, as no clergyman was near enough to be called in time.

At length she spoke. 'Oh, sir, I had a husband, who was a negro, and I fear, a bad man. He died in Lancaster Castle; and, oh, sir, I was sitting one night in a room of the Castle when my husband's head came out of the floor, and seemed to ask me to help him. And then, sir, the devil came through the door, snatched up the head, put it in a bag and disappeared before I could do anything. And I've never done anything. Oh, sir, what can I do for my poor husband's soul?'

CHAPTER V

There now follows exerpts from the booklet mentioned in the early part of this book that details some of the inmates, hangings and punishments of the day entitled: 'The Gossiping Booklet about Lancaster Castle'

On the east-side of the terrace steps will be observed a semi-circular projecting portion in the corner, with dark, fatal, "death's doors,' through which many, sadly too many, criminals have passed to pay the penalty of their guilt upon the black scaffold, which, when executions were conducted in public, was erected in this corner, upon the ground now partly railed off. Standing upon this spot, our mind naturally reverts to the period when executions took place here. It is four o'clock on a Monday morning.

The sky is black as pitch, and the raw, damp air seems to penetrate to the very bones. All is coldness, dreariness, desolation, but withal, animation. The road up Church Street and Castle Hill, along the Terrace, round by the Parade, streams with people; boys and men, and women, some with infants at their breasts pass lightly on, laughing, talking, as to a merry-making, a holiday. All the space hereabouts, from the Church steps to the wall on the Parade, and a large part of the churchyard, is rapidly filling with this motley crowd. The trees that overhang from the churchyard and those on the Parade, are cracking and swaying to and fro with their burden of eager and restless men and lads. Since midnight the workmen have been busy, by the dim light of several miserable lanterns, fixing together the "national platform," and the sound of their hammers (for they have not yet quite finished), mingled with the noise of the crowd, rings jarringly upon the ear.

Four long hours yet before the ceremony begins, and the noise increases with the crowd. Amid the din of the multitude, the yelling, the hooting, the singing, and the "chaffing," may now and again be heard the voices of the local preachers, each striving with all the eloquence and all the voice he can command, to improve the occasion by enforcing a timely warning from the example so shortly to appear. But hark! It is eight bells by the Church clock; and the dismal tolling of the Castle bell announces in unmistakable language that the hour has come.

"Hats off-down there! you with the broad brim-you in the white hat and crape bonnet him!-silence!"

The fatal doors swing open, and-

"Oh, Lord! Oh, Lord!" exclaims a woman, "there's the parson!" "One two-there's Jack! God bless him!"

"How lovely he looks!"

"Drest as if for a wedding!" sobs a woman. "And there's Tom! he sees me he sees me-God be with you, Tom!" "And God

52

will bless 'em all!" cries another female, bursting into tears.

"Why there's only four!" remarks a spectator, with a whining tone of disappointment.

"There must be six," says another, "six was the number."

"But there's only strings for four."

"Then two's been reprieved."

"He's shaking their hands! The Lord bless 'em!"

"How Tom stands! Like a rock! What pluck! Doesn't shake a finger. Keep up, Tom !"

"He's gone below," cries a woman, her voice suddenly husky, and fixing her nails like a beast of prey in the arm of her companion he's gone to draw t' bolt!"

"God bless 'em! God bless 'em !"

A jarring sound a fall, a loud groan, sounding of hate and horror from a thousand hearts-now the shrieks and screams of women, and now the silence of the tomb.

The gallows is again empty; justice is satisfied; the last dread sentence of the law has been carried out, and the crowd gradually disperses.

Debtors

The debtor's side was generally termed by the wags, 'half-crown side,' and was familiarly spoken of as 'Hansbrow's Hotel.'

Previous to the passing of the Bankruptcy Act of 1869, Lancaster Castle was a household word in the mouths of hundreds of families whose only crime-black enough, no doubt was that they were unable to pay twenty shillings in the pound.

Nearly 400 heads of families, arrested at the instance of their creditors, have been incarcerated within its walls at one time. In this mass of human beings every grade of society was to be found, from the once wealthy trader to the humble shopkeeper. Persons have been confined here for debt for a period of over twenty-one years!

The manner of living followed by the debtors shut up in the Castle resembled in many respects that which we read of in writers of the last century, such as Fielding, Smollet, Goldsmith, and others, who have given us glimpses of life among the impecunious dwellers in the old Fleet Prison, at London.

Any debtor who could afford it, was at liberty to 'find himself' the county provided him lodging. There were no less than twenty-two rooms set apart for the accommodation of debtors twenty for males and two for females.

Every debtor on entering the prison was charged a certain sum, termed "room-money," which covered the cost of fire, candles, the use of culinary utensils, etc., during the whole period of his imprisonment, no matter how long. The money was collected by the "roomsmen," who had charge of the rooms, did the cooking, cleaning, etc., and waited upon the debtors in their respective apartments.

The fee varied with the accommodation; from thirty shillings, the highest sum, to five shillings, the lowest. The most expensive room was that 'clept. 'The Snug.' then followed 'The Quaker's,' 'The Tap,' 'The Well Tower,' 'Long Room,' 'Pin Box,' etc., and the cheapest was 'The Constable's.' The latter was used wholly by poor debtors, of which class there were often as many as forty or fifty, all of different tastes and habits. In one of the windows might have been seen an industrious cobbler, plying his avocation, and in another, an unfortunate snip. But these were exceptions; the majority passed their time in hunger and idleness; for if a debtor was too poor to provide for himself, or had no friends outside to help him, he had to be content with prison diet, which cost him nothing, and never disordered his stomach.

Subject to certain regulations, any tradesman in the town had full liberty, at stated times of the day, to convey eatables and drinkables into the Castle for the use of the debtors; and every morning, a miniature market. where butcher's meat, bread, butter, groceries, vegetables, fish, and other commodities might be purchased, was held in the Castle-yard. Bottled ale might be taken in to a limited extent, but spirits were prohibited under a heavy penalty, and tobacco, though at one time allowed, was also forbidden, to the utter discomfiture of those who, when outside, declared they could not live a week without it, and who found partial solace for lack of 'pigtail' in chewing immoderate quantities of Spanish liquorice.

Many of the richer debtors were regular subscribers to the daily newspapers; and it was the duty of the writer of this, when a lad, to distribute those papers among the debtors for his master twice daily. One wealthy debtor, who spent fifteen years of his life in the Castle, took two Manchester, one Liverpool, and two London papers daily; and on Saturdays, two illustrated papers, a review, a six-penny sporting paper, and several weeklies besides. Many others bought the papers at irregular intervals, and passed them on to their poorer comrades when they had done with them; so they were all well posted up in the news of the day, and not a few took a keen interest in the sporting articles.

To soften the rigours of incarceration and pass the time away every sort of amusement was invented, such as mock elections, race running round the yard, cards, dominoes, skittles, amateur theatricals, and dancing. It not unfrequently occurred that there were several debtors confined at one time who were good players on the violin, banjo, flute, or other musical instrument. When this was the case, couples were formed in the yard, where dancing was kept up till bed-time.

Imprisonment for debt is a thing of the past; but while it lasted and it was a time-honoured institution it had its lights and shades. With all its apparent pleasures to the casual visitor, with all its outward signs of jollity and reckless mirth, it was very little better than hell itself to eight out of every ten of its unfortunate victims. Many a poor wretch has been torn from his suffering family at a moment perhaps the most un-prepared, who, when imprisoned, spent sleepless nights, depending on the issue of his bail; day after day, week after week, there was nought but disappointment, oppression, and injustice. during which time his beloved wife and family were suffering absolute starvation, unprotected, and unfriended.

CHAPTER VI

*Gallows Hill – The Hangings – The Hangmen – The Tower
Instruments of correction – The Court – The Drop Room*

In the year 1784, the business of two assizes was removed from the Castle to the Town Hall, in consequence of a terrible fever the result of the wretched dietary and insanitary conditions of that time breaking out in the Castle, which carried off great numbers. With that exception assizes have been held regularly within its walls twice a year for a period of over six hundred and thirty years.

A great French writer of the last century observes that England, more than any other country, has been distinguished for the stern delight of slaughtering men with the pretended sword of the law, and that the history of England ought to be written by

the executioner. And if it is true that a nation becomes more humane as it grows more intelligent, the remark of Dr. Johnson to the young aristocrat who was boasting of his long line of ancestors, was not said without due regard to historical facts: "A wise man never attempts to trace his genealogy too far back, because if he do, he is sure to run upon an ancestor who has been hanged." From the year 1800 to 1887, no fewer than 228 persons have been strangled, 'according to law,' at the Castle of Lancaster!

Prior to the year 1800, the execution of criminals took place on the Moor, a little above where Christ Church now stands, and opposite the southern entrance to the Williamson Park.

The spot, which is at present marked by a stone seat, was well known as Gallows Hill, and commands a view of some of the grandest scenery in England. Here the gallows, of the old Tyburn pattern[12], was erected, surrounded by a line of javelin men, who kept off the crowd previous to and after the arrival of the victims.

As the crowd advanced up Moor Lane and through Moor Gate, the whistling, singing, and shouting which usually accompanies a mob, announced that the cortège with the prisoner was in sight. Seated in a cart by the side of his coffin, was the culprit, a guard of halberdiers[13] following, while an

12 The Tyburn gallows, commonly known as Tyburn Tree, was triangular in plan, with three uprights and three crossbeams, allowing up to 24 people to be executed simultaneously when all three sides were used.
13 The halberd consists of an axe blade topped with a spike mounted on a long shaft. It can have a hook or thorn on the back side of the axe blade. The halberd was usually 4.9 to 5.9 ft long. Troops that used the weapon were called halberdiers.

escort went in front and opened out the road through the crowd of sightseers.

On arriving at the top of the hill, the cart would halt beneath the gallows, and the hangman would jump in and adjust the rope round the neck of the criminal. At the signal, "Drive on!" the cart left the victim swinging in the air; and thus the sentence of the law- "You shall hang by the neck until you are dead" was carried out in its strict literal sense, the sufferer dying by sheer strangulation, and not instantaneously killed by breaking the neck, as at present more mercifully substituted. There are forty-eight executions recorded as having taken place on Gallows Hill* between the years 1782 and 1799.

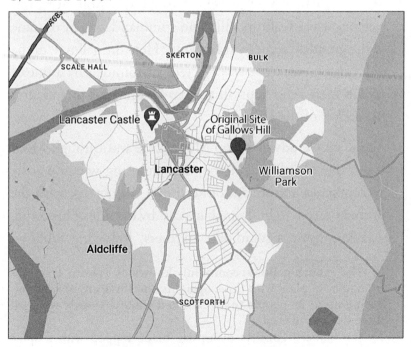

Original site of *Gallows Hill

Map Extract taken from Google Maps (a trademark of Google LLC)

The Hangings

In the year 1793, one of the most painful executions that ever occurred took place here. The whole of the circumstances were of a heartrending nature, not only on account of the man being executed innocently, but from the fact of the trial, the conviction, and the legal murder of this unhappy victim being attributable to a woman's fury.

The facts are briefly these:- Joseph Clark, a rather superior young man, said to be well-read, a splendid player on the violin, and otherwise exceedingly agreeable, was beloved by a married lady living near his own house, and to whose house he often went in the capacity of lover to her servant-maid.

One Sunday morning, on her return from church, she caught her maid in the bedroom with Clark, and became so enraged with jealousy that she caused her servant to swear a rape against him. This was accordingly done; and, strange to relate, he was condemned principally on the evidence, not of the girl herself, but of her mistress.

The greatest excitement prevailed on the day of the trial, as it was generally believed that he was innocent; and so certain were his friends of his acquittal, that a conveyance was in waiting, with a change of clothing, during his trial. When the jury pronounced him guilty, he fell prostrate at the bar, exclaiming, "Oh, God, I am a murdered man!" Every possible means were taken to save him; but all was of no avail. He was hanged on Gallows Hill, and a death-bed confession, made many years after by his wretched persecutor, proved that he was hanged innocently.

Alas! the love of woman! it is known

To be a lovely and a fearful thing:

For all of theirs upon that die is thrown,

And if 'tis lost, life hath no more to bring

To them but mockeries of the past alone;

And their revenge is, as the tiger's spring,

Deadly, and quick, and crushing; yet as real

Torture is theirs; what they inflict they feel.

The year 1794 was a most extraordinary one in the annals of Lancaster Castle, for there was not a single execution, a circumstance that had not been previously known to the oldest inhabitant.

In 1797, Samuel Longworth, convicted of murdering a young man named Horrocks, at Dean, near Bolton, was hung at Lancaster, and his body gibbeted for two months on Dean Moor. His remains, which were afterwards buried at the foot of the gibbet, were discovered on the spot so lately as 1887. With reference to this gruesome subject, a lady at Radcliffe writes:-

My grandmother, with her parents, brothers and sisters, lived at Atherton, and farmed land, I believe, belonging to the owner of Atherton Hall. They took their produce to Liverpool, bringing back such things as they might require. During the years that the pressgang struck terror throughout the country, neither her father nor brothers dared go to Liverpool, so my grandmother, or mother, or her sisters had to go. On May 28th 1797, it was grandmother's turn to go to Liverpool. She, as was the custom with some women, tied a handkerchief on her head, and put on a tall hat belonging to one of her brothers, and taking a horse and cart and what she had to sell, set out early, passing the gibbet on Dean Moor on her way. She did her business in Liverpool, but it was rather late when she set out on her return, and it was near midnight when she got back in sight of the gibbet. The corpse was still there, and under the gibbet were two men. On hearing the cart they went to it and stopped the horse. They asked her if she had seen them at the gibbet. She replied that she had, and they said they should take her life as then she could tell no tales. However, one of the men took his companion aside, and they whispered together, after which they asked her name, where she lived, and what family her father and mother had. They said they would let her go if she would promise never to tell what she had seen, but if she did tell they would murder her and all her family, Of course she promised, and they let her go. She managed to get home, but fainted at the door, and was ill for some time after. She heard from the family that the corpse was gone next day. Whether the authorities had had it cut down, or the two men had stolen it, she dared not ask; but the events of that night clung to her like some fearful dream. She soon after married and came to Radcliffe, and I don't think she ever knew the upshot of the affair.

This explains why Longworth's remains were found under the gibbet. The two men were undoubtedly the former companions of the gibbeted man, and, out of sheer sympathy, had cut down the body, and buried it at this unearthly hour, on the spot where the remains were so recently found.

In the year 1799, the last execution took place on Gallows Hill. Ever since, all executions have taken place at the Castle. A remarkable circumstance occurred at this execution, viz., an attempt to save the life of the culprit, whose name was James Case, a surgeon, condemned to death for 'making bad notes,' It was discovered after his execution that a small pipe had been introduced into his throat, and that he had also worked the knot of the rope as much under his chin as possible. The coffin, which his friends had provided, was found to be perforated with small holes at both sides and the ends, in anticipation that he would save himself by the means already mentioned. However, all failed, for the poor fellow when cut down was quite dead.

At the August Assizes of 1801, there were eight condemned and executed, two of them for uttering forged notes, one for stealing printed calico, one for highway robbery, one for attempting to seduce a soldier from his duty, and three (brothers) for burglary, altogether there were eighteen persons hanged behind the Castle in the first year of the last century- seven (including two brothers) on Saturday, April 25th, three (one of them a woman) a week afterwards, and sight on September 12th. Until that year there had not been a woman executed at Lancaster since 1772, when Mary

CHAPTER VI

Hilton was hanged and burnt for poisoning her husband at Middle Hulton, near Bolton. None of the eighteen who suffered the death penalty in 1801 had committed murder. The culprit who endeavoured to seduce a soldier from his duty left behind him a confession, which bears marks of the kindly assistance of the prison chaplain. It runs thus:-

I William Gallant, a native of Bolton, born to a humble but respectable station in life, now only twenty-three years of age, am going to be taken out of that society with ignominy, in which, if I had chosen, I might have lived with comfort and credit. Instead of sticking to my business as a weaver of cloths, I thought of nothing but weaving and unweaving Governments. A paper was put into my hands, which I to give to those whom I thought ripe for rebellion. It was agreed to attempt to seduce the Army and Navy first Part of the 17th Regiment of Light Dragoons being at that time quartered at Bolton, I began to tamper with two of the soldiers, and as soon as I conceived them prepared to join us, I disclosed to them our object and the means we proposed to accomplish it. God Almighty grant that my miserable end may have its due effect on those deluded people who forsake their homes and peaceable callings to engage in plots, in which, if they are successful, I am now convinced would only increase instead of diminish any imaginary hardships. You who are spectators of this dreadful catastrophe, and you who shall hereafter read of it, take an important lesson. Follow the precept of the Holy Apostle; study to be quiet, and to do your own business, and to work with your own hands.

At the March assizes, 1803, George Short was hanged for sheep stealing, and four other prisoners suffered the same fate for burglary. Two others, charged with manslaughter, were ordered to be burnt in the hand, and suffer twelve months' imprisonment.

It has been truly observed that custom renders all men indifferent to the sufferings of their fellow-creatures. In the old Roman days men were crucified so often that it ceased even to be a show; the soldiers played at dice under the miserable wretches, the peasant women stepping by jested and laughed and sang. Almost in our own time, dry skeletons creaked on gibbets at every cross road, when for thirty shillings men were hung. And the thirst for blood grow stronger, Men's lives were valued then at a sheep's Thank God that lasts no longer.

"So strong is custom and tradition, and the habit of thought it weaves about us," says Richard Jefferies, "that I have heard ancient and grave farmers, when the fact was mentioned with horror, hum and ha, and stroke their beards, and mutter that they didn't know as 'twas altogether such a bad thing as they was hung for sheep-stealing."

At the summer assizes of 1803, three lads not exceeding 17 years of age, were executed, two of whom were charged with burglary and one with forgery.

The late Sergeant Ballantine relates an anecdote that exemplifies a state of the criminal law existing at this period, which in these days almost defies belief. He says: "Bristol possessed a recorder Sir Robert Gifford a man of great eminence, and the court over which he presided had jurisdiction in capital cases. A friend of mine was present, when a boy, scarcely more than a child, was prosecuted for passing a forged one pound Bank of England note. At this time doubtless these were largely circulated through the country, and the tradespeople, of whom the juries were composed, suffered greatly by the traffic. The recorder summed up strongly for an acquittal, upon the ground that no guilty knowledge was shown, but the jury convicted. The recorder was much affected, and leaned over to the solicitor who appeared for the Bank, and my friend heard him say, "For God's sake, save this poor boy's life!" If any response was made, it was not an affirmative one, and the boy was hung." He adds: "Do my readers recollect a most affecting description written by Thackeray in his sketch of Dr. Dodd's execution, of a child carried to Tyburn in the same vehicle with the doctor, the mother clinging to it, weeping over her offspring, the victim of the same barbarous law and of merciless statesmen?" On the 9th April, 1808, Mary Charnley, 19 years of wars of age, was executed behind the Castle, for the crime of robbing her master's house at Liverpool.

At the March assizes of 1805, John Lever was tried before Baron Graham for the wilful murder of his wife's uncle, aged 82, at Radcliffe. He was found guilty and sentenced to death, and his body afterwards to be dissected and anatomised, which sentence was carried into effect on Monday, the 1st of April.

At this period the law did not allow the sun to set a second time upon a murderer after he was convicted, unless a Sunday intervened. Hence it was usual for the judges to try such cases on the Friday, in order that the criminal might have the longest time allowed by law. The execution of murderers generally took place then at eight o'clock on a Monday morning.

At the March assizes, 1809, seven men, all charged with uttering forged notes, were executed at one time; and at the following assizes, in September, six others, for the same offence, met a similar fate, making thirteen for the two assizes. During the first thirty years of the leat century, no fewer than 53 persons were hanged behind Lancaster Castle for attempting to pass bad notes.

In May, 1812, rioting took place in several parts of the county, and 25 men and women, charged with this offence in Manchester, Middleton, and Ashton-under-Lyne, were brought to the Castle, escorted by a troop of Scots Greys[14].

A special Commission for their trial was opened on the 23rd, and on the 13th of the following month, seven men and one woman were executed for taking part in it. One of these was a youth, not 16 years of age, who cried piteously on the scaffold for his mother to save him. A company of infantry attended the executions. At the August assizes of the same year, a military officer, of noble connections, was executed for forgery. His name was Sloane, though executed in the name of Wright. He was a personal friend of the Prince Regent, and letters to that effect were handed to the jury;

---

14 The Royal Scots Greys was a cavalry regiment of the British Army from 1707 until 1971

but all was of no avail, though immense sums were expended in the endeavour to save him. It was said that a moderate fortune was spent in this unfortunate man's interest.

At the March Assizes of 1814, Benjamin Butterworth, James Ashworth, and Charles Taylor, were executed for burglary. When they were being tied up, Taylor called out, "Now, lads, kick off your shoes," which they did.

At the autumn assizes of 1816, no fewer than 31 prisoners were sentenced to death, but 24 were respited. Among those left for execution was a woman, named Susannah Holroyd, condemned for the murder of her husband. She was executed on the 16th of September, and her body afterwards handed over to the surgeons for dissection.

On the 19th April, 1817, nine prisoners were executed on the same scaffold at one time behind the Castle, and not one of this number for any greater crime than that of highway robbery, and four of them were under 20 years of age.

The highway robber of this period seems to have occupied relatively the same position to the "highwayman" as the petty thief of the present day does to the "defaulter." The highway robber had his life cut short by the executioner; the highwayman had his life and exploits commemorated by the novelist. The former bluntly demanded your money or your life"; the latter, like Claude Duval, for instance, went about the business in a more polite manner; he simply "exacted contributions."

At the March Assizes of 1818 there were 128 prisoners for trial, no less than 49 of whom were sentenced to death, but only the following were left for execution:-W. Stewart, T. Curry, Margaret Dowd, and Robt. Wardlow, for uttering forged notes, and George Hesketh, for burglary.

At the Quarter Sessions held at the Castle on October 20th, in the same year, Thomas Patten was convicted of having in his possession certain machinery used in the cotton manufacture of this kingdom, with intent to export the same to America, and was sentenced to be imprisoned for 12 months in the Castle, pay a fine of £200, and be further imprisoned until such fine was paid, and the goods to be forfeited.

At the March Assizes of 1819, no less than 44 men were sentenced to death, and six were left without any hope of a remission of the sentence. four for uttering forged notes, one for rape, and one for burglary.

From this period down to the year 1827, there appears to be nothing of interest in the painful history of this part of our Castle associations, except, perhaps, the execution of James Ashcroft, senior, David Ashcroft, James Ashcroft, junior, and William Holden, when there was very great excitement in the county for a long period, in consequence of the very general belief in their innocence. The execution of these men (father, brother, son, and son-in-law) took place on the 8th September, 1817, for murder and robbery at the house of Mr. Littlewood, Pendleton, near Manchester. The poor fellows continued to declare their innocence to the last moment. William Holden was the first on the scaffold. He appeared quite composed, and addressed the crowd in these words:-

CHAPTER VI

Strangers and neighbours, friends and relatives and foreigners; I am now going to meet my God, and in the face of Him I declare that I am as innocent of the concern as the child unborn, and hope that the Lord in heaven will be merciful to my poor soul for all my former sins. Dear friends, I could tell you no more if I was to talk to you all day. The Lord bless you, for the Lord Jesus knows I forgive everyone that has sworn my life away. The Lord receive my soul. I have been a very wicked man.

David Ashcroft next stepped forward, and avowed his innocence in the strongest possible terms, after which Holden again came forward, and said:

I declare I left them at half-past two o'clock, and I believe they are all as I am.

James Ashcroft, junior, then prayed as follows:-

Thou knows, O Lord, we are not deserving of this; Thou knows we are innocent.

He then asked for his father, who was led on the scaffold just at this time, and embraced him. James Ashcroft, senior, then turned to the spectators, and in the most solemn manner ex- claimed, "I declare we are all innocent!" While they were being tied up, they all joined in singing a hymn, the words of which David Ashcroft gave out thus:-

I'll praise my Maker whilst I've breath;

And when my voice is lost in death,

Praise shall employ my nobler powers;

My days of praise shall ne'er be past,

While life, and thought, and being last,

71

Or immortality endures.

Happy the man whose hopes rely

On Israel's God.

At this point the bolt was drawn, and, whether innocent or guilty and it was a matter of precious little moment in those days, no time being allowed for further inquiry, they were strangled, and their bodies handed over to the surgeons for dissection. After these executions, nothing could appease the popular excitement, which was kept alive for upwards of twelve months, every one being satisfied of the innocence of these unfortunate men.

At the autumn assizes of 1827, a father and his two sons were executed for highway robbery and burglary.

At the spring assizes of 1830, Paul Rigby, John Grimes, and Mary Grimes, were condemned to death for highway robbery with violence, at Scotforth, near Lancaster. A scoundrel, named Stanley, swore that the prisoners first bound him fast to a gate (a position in which he was actually found), and then robbed him of a considerable sum of money. Through the exertions of the chaplain, it discovered only was a few hours before the execution should have taken place, the gallows being in readiness- that Stanley had committed a terrible perjury, and that the charge he had preferred against the prisoners was a fabrication, thetic arranged for the purpose of obtaining money from sympathetic persons. The prisoners were in due time liberated, and as a solution for the mental anguish they must have endured, their coffins, which had been duly prepared for their dead bodies, were handed to them when they left the Castle. The Grimes did not long keep possession of theirs; but Rigby took his home to Blackburn, and made a neat corner cupboard of it.

William Worrall, executed March, 1831, deliberately kicked off his shoes on the scaffold, to give the lie to his mother, who had often told him that unless he improved his conduct he would never die with his shoes off a significant hint that he would terminate his career on the gallows.

At the March assizes of 1832, two men, named Heaton and Thomas, were convicted of murder and sentenced to death. There were 43 other prisoners sentenced to death at these assizes for various offences, but their sentences were afterwards commuted- 37 were transported for life, 1 for 14 years, 3 for 7 years, and the others to short terms of imprisonment. Heaton and Thomas were executed on the 12th March, and their bodies ordered to be given to the surgeons for dissection. The body of Heaton was sent to the surgeons at Warrington, and that of Thomas to Liverpool.

At the August assizes of 1832, Mr. Justice Parke, in his charge to the Grand Jury, stated that two Acts had recently been passed-one abrogating the punishment of death in all cases connected with the counterfeiting of the current coin of the realm, and making the punishment mt either transportation for life or imprisonment with hard labour, at the discretion of the Judge. By the other Act the punishment of death was abrogated in all cases of cattle stealing, or stealing in a dwelling- house to the value of £5, but making the punishment in all cases transportation for life. The bodies of murderers were no longer to be anatomised or hung in chains, but to be buried in the precincts of the prison in which they were last confined. More recent executions, but without any special circumstances attending them, are as follows:- August 25th, 1853, Richard Pedder, for the murder of his wife at Hambleton, near Garstang.

August 29th, 1857, Richard Hardman, for wife murder at Chorley. In 1862, Walker Moore, a tailor at Colne, murdered his wife by cutting her throat, and was sentenced to death at the August assizes in the same year. The prisoner, during his trial, was peculiarly defiant and insolent, and it is stated that he had declared that the rope was not made that would hang him. His execution was fixed for the 30th of August, and the scaffold was erected as usual during the night outside the prison. In the morning, between seven and sight o'clock, the condemned man asked permission to go to the water closet, and it was of course granted. He appears to have at once pulled off his clogs, and swung himself up into the water cistern-a large one for the supply of several closets. He was found face downwards in the water of this cistern a few minutes afterwards dead. The consternation among the officials of the prison at this deliberate and determined suicide may be imagined. When the fact became known outside that Moore had avoided death on the scaffold by drowning himself a few minutes before the hour fixed for his execution, the excitement was immense. The churchyard, the Parade, and all the grounds adjacent to the prison were crowded by thousands of people, many of whom had walked all night from Colne and neighbourhood. The crowds lingered for hours around the scaffold, expecting to see the dead body of Moore formally suspended from the beam, and there were frequent cries of "Bring him out!" The multitude, however, were disappointed in this demand, and Moore remained unhanged.

March 25th, 1865, Stephen Burke, for wife murder at Preston. This was the last public execution at the Castle. In 1868, an Act was passed prohibiting public executions[15], and directing that all executions take place inside the walls of the prison, in presence of the sheriff, gaoler, chaplain, and surgeons of the prison, and such others as the sheriff requires or allows. The Act further orders that executions shall take place at 8 a.m. on the first Monday after the intervention of three Sundays from the day of which sentence is passed.

These were the first executions in Lancaster, after the passing of the Act above named.

August 16th, 1875, Mark Fidler, for wife murder at Preston; and William M'Cullough, for the murder of William Watson, at Barrow.

February 11, 1879, William M'Guinness, for wife murder at Barrow.

---

15 The Capital Punishment Amendment Act 1868 received royal assent on 29 May 1868, putting an end to public executions for murder in the United Kingdom. The act required that all prisoners sentenced to death for murder be executed within the walls of the prison in which they were being held, and that their bodies be buried in the prison grounds. It was prompted at least in part by the efforts of reformers such as Sir Robert Peel and Charles Dickens, who called in the national press for an end to the "grotesque spectacle" of public executions.

February 9th, 1886, Joseph Baines, for wife murder at Barrow.

August 1st, 1887, Alfred Sowrey, for the murder of his sweetheart, Annie Kelly, at Preston.

November 16th, 1910, Thomas Rawcliffe, for wife murder at Lancaster.

From the year 1799 to 1887 inclusive, there have been 228 persons executed at the Castle of Lancaster, 170 of whom were attended on the scaffold by one chaplain, the Rev. J. Rowley, who filled that office for over half-a-century. Putting aside the murderers, how dreadful to reflect on the past when we consider the large number of poor  creatures who have been put to death for offences which at this day would be met by only a few weeks' imprisonment.

The Hangmen

Out of the 228 criminals who paid the death penalty, 131 were executed by one hangman, named Edward Barlow, a Welshman, commonly called Old Ned. It is said that he was a greater villain than any man he ever put to death.

He was several times convicted, and twice sentenced to transportation. He officiated as executioner to nine at the same moment, which was the greatest number he ever "turned off" at one time. This occurred on the 19th of April, 1817. His poor victims-four of whom were under 20 years of age hung so closely together that they jostled one another on the drop. We are told the sight was harrowing to the last degree.

Barlow led a wretched life; there were very few houses in which he was permitted to enter; many times he was seriously abused, and pelted with missiles of the foulest description; yet he maintained his post, with little intermission, for a period of thirty years. He died in the Castle, and was succeeded by Calcraft[16], certainly a more respectable individual, and one who showed some little consideration for his victims.

---

16 William Calcraft (11 October 1800 – 13 December 1879) was a 19th-century English hangman, one of the most prolific of British executioners. It is estimated in his 45-year career he carried out 450 executions. A cobbler by trade, Calcraft was initially recruited to flog juvenile offenders held in Newgate Prison. While selling meat pies on streets around the prison, Calcraft met the City of London's hangman, John Foxton.

Of all modern hangmen, Calcraft was perhaps the most widely known. A man of about middle height, of a stout, heavy build, and rather intelligent features, he could converse with a friend or a stranger in as gentlemanly a manner as could be desired. His conversational abilities, though to a great degree tinctured with matter not usually brought forward in the polite circles of society, were neither low -saving the matter or subject of conversation-nor vulgar; and he could tell many a queer anecdote respecting certain of his "subjects" in a quiet, humorous, and sometimes satirical manner. Many years ago, we remember, he presided at the breakfast table soon after a double execution, when the

conversation the circle being select, numbering not more than six-naturally turned upon the event just accomplished, and respecting which he was not at all disinclined to speak. "What do you think of the two criminals executed this morning?" asked one.

Well (this very deliberately), I never attended any with more melancholy pleasure in my whole experience. They were really first-rate plucky fellows. Stood to the last with downright courage." "Better than Hackett, at Exeter, the other day?"

"He was certainly very good, and behaved well. Gentlemen, you must know that one of the ropes I used to-day has been round more than twenty persons' necks."

"Indeed," says one, "do you value it, or is it of a particular kind."

Mr. Calcraft, however, gave no information as "to its particularity", he only added that amongst others it was used for Manning said some one, "Manning was a Somersetshire man."

"Indeed; very well," continued the great authority, "Manning was a great muff; Manning was a regular coward. What an awful fright he was in to be sure! How he shook when the rope was going round his neck!" (Some of the company looked as if they should probably follow the muff's example.) "But the wife was first-rate; stood as firm as a rock; never flinched; took it as if it was nothing of any great consequence. But as for him -pooh!"

"Do you recollect Sarah Harriet Thomas, at Bristol, for the murder of her mistress, Miss Jeffreys?"

"Ah! she was hung the day before Rush; poor, poor thing! (Something like a sigh escaped from him.) Thirty-three years I have followed this concern, but she was the worst I ever met. She was really dreadful; though she was a pretty girl very good-looking face. How she did cry out, to be sure! She would not sit to be pinioned. Her's and Rush's affairs were two days' hard work." "Rush," says one, "was a notorious fellow."

"Wasn't he!" said the hangman, "but very plucky. He leserved his fate"-a proposition assented to by all present. Much conversation of the same kind followed, and then reverted to the two "subjects" he had despatched that morning.

"Do you think they died quickly?"

"Death, you may say from me, was instantaneous. There was no struggle. Death seemed to have no soreness for them.

I didn't tie their legs." "How did they conduct themselves before appearing on the drop?

"Oh, very well indeed, especially the soldier. By-the-bye, he wore a medal; but it seems he willed it to the priest that priest was a very nice sort of man who visited him; and as I like to act fairly though you know it was my property why, I took it off, gave it to the governor, who in turn gave it to the priest. I wouldn't do anything wrong on any account, and as it was his last wish why, there, poor fellow!'"

"Perhaps you can decide a point my friend and I were

in doubt upon this morning: What are the sensations of condemned criminals previous to taking the final plunge?"

"Well, I have heard it said, that when you are tied up, and your face turned towards the Castle wall, you see its stones expanding and contracting violently, and a similar expansion and contraction seem to take place in your own head and breast. Then there is a rush of fire and an earthquake; your eye-balls spring out of their sockets; the Castle shoots up into the air, and you tumble down a precipice!" "That is a very strong description, sir."

"And a no less strong sensation, I do assure you," returned Calcraft, who apologising for his abrupt departure, as he had to catch the London train, shook hands all round and withdrew.

Calcraft retired in 1874, after nearly 40 years' service, when Marwood, the originator of the long drop, was appointed to the office, who, dying in 1883, was followed by Binns. Berry and then Billington.

The Tower

It has been decided to gather together all the antiquities belonging to the Castle, and place them in this tower, thus making a sort of museum of it. The thickness of the wall is nine feet five inches, and the age of the masonry is supposed to be upwards of 1,700 years. That the wall is Roman, there is no shadow of doubt. It appears to have been built after the usual Roman manner, the stones (principally blue cobbles from the seashore) having been put together loosely and then the cement poured upon them, a building system called 'grouting'.

After cutting through the wall, the masons, quite unexpectedly, broke into an old dungeon, which was found

to be filled up with earth; this was, of course, dug out, and at the further end was discovered the old oaken door, apparently in good preservation, hanging on its hinges. Unfortunately, it fell into pieces due to age and decay when trying to lift the door from its hinges. The remains, however, have been carefully preserved and are shown to visitors along with the enormous hinges and bolts. Using an old plan lately brought to light, it has since been ascertained that this dungeon is one of six that form the basement of the old Crown Court. They appear to have been when a portion of the castle was set apart for the confinement of lunatics.

There are still the remains of the holdfasts in the dungeon's walls, to which the prisoners were chained, and it is obvious to anyone that in this cell, there would be an entire absence of light and ventilation.

Having passed through the thickness of the old wall and the dungeon, we find ourselves in Adrian's Tower. This tower the outside of which has been cased with blocks of ashlar[17], to be in character with the modern parts of the Castle, was built by order of the Emperor Adrian in the year 124. It is circular in shape, with walls nearly eight feet thick. At the time of the Romans, the lower portion, which has only recently been excavated, was used as a mill, in which the corn was ground for the garrison; and in the time of John o'Gaunt, it was the bakery, and called "The Oven." Afterwards, it seems to have fallen somewhat into decay, and the floor had been raised some six or eight feet, but in the year 1810, the upper portion was made into a Record Room, in which the records and documents belonging to the duchy were kept. These had been removed from the Castle some years ago, and the authorities having no further use for the room, it was decided to pull down the cupboards,

---

17 A type of masonry that requires only a little mortar to bind it. The term can refer either to an individual stone that has been "finely dressed" (cut and worked) until squared off, or to a structure built from such stones.

excavate the interior, and restore the lower portion to its original character.

In taking away one of these cupboards, a manuscript was discovered, folded up and nailed down to the top of it. This has been placed on view, so that both sides of the paper may be read. The following is a literal copy of one side of the sheet :

This is to inform the generations to come that this Record Room was finished on the 14th day of May 1810 49 year of George III. The Local militia was assembled at this time at Lancaster for 20 days. Sir Francis Burdett was a prisoner in the tower for standing up for the rights of the people. Provisions of all sorts high and working people very poor. Napoleon, Emperor of the French, had all the nations of Europe either in subjection or alliance against England, divorced his first wife, who was the widow of a French general and now he has married the daughter of Francis II Emperor of Austria which has been sixteen years at war with the french.

The reverse side displays an old constable's report, which is crossed out by the joiners as af no account. It reads thus :-

Clayton-le-Woods in the parish of Leyland in the County of Lancaster, August 3rd, 1807. This is to certify the Honourable Bench at the General Assizes holden at the Castle in Lancaster, August 8th, 1807, that as our highways are in good repair, our poor well provided for, have nothing at this time to present by me.

RICHARD BRIGHOUSE, Constable.

To Mr.

HIS MAJESTY having ordered the Right Honorable EDWARD EARL OF DERBY, the Lord Lieutenant of the County of *Lancaster*, to call out the LOCAL MILITIA of the same County, for the purpose of being trained and exercised,

NOTICE

IS HEREBY GIVEN YOU.

That you (being enrolled to serve in the Lonsdale Regiment of Lancashire Local Militia) are to appear at *Lancaster* in the said County, on Monday the 29th Day of MAY, instant, at 10 o'Clock in the Forenoon, then and there to hold yourself in every Respect ready to be trained and exercised for a Time not exceeding 28 Days, and to behave as the Laws of your Country in general, and those of the Local Militia in particular direct. And you are to take further Notice, that in Case you neglect to appear at the Time and Place aforesaid, you will be considered as a Deserter, and Punished as such. Given under my Hand the 23*d.* Day of MAY, 1809.

Edward Bramwell, Constable of Ulverston.

O. ASHBURNER, PRINTER, ULVERSTON.

Instruments of correction

On the walls are placed three pikes, taken from the Scottish rebels at Preston in 1715, by the Lancashire Regiment of Militia; a number of brass candlesticks, dated 1743, used in the Crown Court before the introduction of gas, and a variety of shackles and handcuffs, comprising the 'heavy double irons,' the 'double irons,' the 'basil,' 'shackle bolt handcuffs' 'letter B handcuffs,' 'rivet cuffs,' 'figure of 8 cuffs,' and various other body and leg irons.

Before the introduction of railways, and when Lancaster was the only town in the county in which assizes were held, all prisoners for trial were brought from the remotest parts of the county in coaches or wagons, and the lighter irons here exhibited would be used as a means of preventing their escape. The heavier irons, alas! could they speak, might tell us fearful tales of woe and suffering, which Sterne, in his "Sentimental Journey," can only be said to have faintly outlined in the following extract:-

> *I sat down close by my table, and leaning my head upon my hand, I began to figure to myself the miseries of confinement. I took a single captive; and having first shut him up in his dungeon, I then looked through the twilight of his grated door to take his picture. I beheld*

his body half wasted away with long expectation and confinement, and felt what kind of sickness of the heart it was which arises from hope deferred. Upon looking nearer, I saw him pale and feverish; in thirty years the western breeze had not once fanned his blood; he had seen no sun, no moon, in all that time, nor had the voice of friend or kinsman breathed through his lattice. He was sitting upon the ground on a little straw, in the furthest corner of the dungeon, which was alternately his chair and bed; a little calendar of small sticks was laid at the head, notched all over with the dismal days and nights he had passed there; he had one of these little sticks in his hand, and, with a rusty nail, he was etching another day of misery to add to the heap. As I darkened the little light he had, he lifted up a hopeless eye towards the door, then cast it down, shook his head, and went on with his work of affliction. I heard his chains upon his legs, as he turned his body to lay his little stick upon the bundle. He gave a deep sigh. I saw the iron enter into his soul! I burst into tears. I could not sustain the picture of confinement which my fancy had drawn.

There is also exhibited a Brank, an instrument formerly used for the punishment of scolds, and often called "the scold's bridle," or "gossip's bridle." It was never a legalised instrument of punishment, although corporations, lords of the manor, etc., exercised the right of inflicting such punishment. Men were put in the stocks or pillory, and women in the branks for such petty misdemeanours as using abusive, insulting, or threatening language, swearing, etc. The brank here shown is a hoop of iron, opening by hinges at the sides, so as to enclose the head, and fastened by a staple with a padlock at the back; a plate within the front of the hoop projected inwards, so as to fit into the mouth of the culprit, and by pressing upon the tongue be an effectual gag. In some instances this mouth-plate was armed with a knife or point, which cut the tongue if moved. With this upon her head, the unfortunate woman was paraded through the streets by the bellman, beadle, or constable, or was chained to the market cross, a target for ridicule and insult.

The Brank

Mounted and framed are some fragments which reveal the keen thirst for liberty manifested by their respective owners, and attached to the relics is a label with these words:-

Implements taken from prisoners attempting to escape from Lancaster Castle. Collected by A. Hansbrow, Esq., Deputy Governor. The gift of Colonel Whalley, June, 1891.

The huge wooden chair shown in our illustration was formerly used to strap in and bind violent lunatics. This was at a time previous to the opening of the County Lunatic Asylum, in 1816, when a portion of the Castle was set apart for the confinement of lunatics.

The Court

Owing to the circumstance that until of late years Lancaster was the only town at which assizes were held for the whole county, more persons have been sentenced to death at the bar of this court than in any other court in the kingdom. In the four years 1816-19, no less than 240 persons received sentence of death here; the great majority, however, were reprieved before the judges left town.

In the dock, where prisoners stand to take their trial, is exhibited the holdfast and branding-iron, the latter stamped with the letter M. The prisoner who had had been sentenced to be branded was seized, his left hand thrust into the holdfast, and the iron, after being made red-hot, was pressed against the "brawne of the thumb," and thus he was

Branding with an M for malefactor

branded for life as a malefactor, and effectually prevented from earning an honest livelihood, however desirous he might be of doing so after the term of imprisonment that usually followed, and which was intended to reform him, had expired. The ceremony was performed in open court, in the presence of the judge and jury; and it was customary for the brander, before releasing the hand the hand of the culprit, to survey his work, and, if satisfactory, turn to the judge and pronounce it, "A fair mark, my Lord!" This barbarous form of punishment has been inflicted on this very spot within modern times- in fact, in the year 1803 two men, for manslaughter, were sentenced to twelve months' imprisonment, and were publicly branded. Our boasted civilization is evidently not of so ancient a date as some folks would have us believe. Further, it was then customary for prisoners, when placed in the dock to plead, to hold up the left hand, in order that the Court might see whether a previous conviction had ever been recorded against them. In the account of the life and death of George Marsh, the Lancashire martyr, who was burnt at Chester in 1555, we read that "he was sent to Lancaster Castle, and being brought with other prisoners unto the sessions, was made to hold up his hand with the malefactors." Looking from the bench, this court has a very fine appearance; all the arches recede, and finish with a very beautiful screen of stone-work.

The Drop Room

Before leaving the visitor is favoured with a view of the old drop room, so called because from this room all criminals condemned to death between the years 1800 and 1868 have had to pass, after being piniond therein, to the drop. It was formerly circular in shape and much larger than it is now, a good part having been taken up within the last twenty years by a lavatory, etc., for the use of those having business at the sessions or assizes.

The furniture of this room is extremely meagre, almost the only article deserving that title being a wheeled chair, especially constructed for the conveyance to the scaffold of a notorious criminal, named Jane Scott. This young woman was convicted and sentenced to death, at the March assizes of 1828, for the murder of her mother by poison, at Preston. She was so infirm and broken in health that she could not walk to the scaffold, but was taken thither on this chair, which, when the rope was adjusted, was withdrawn from under her. Her body was afterwards given to the surgeons for dissection.

At the furthest end of the room to the right is a doorway, that communicated with the chapel, through which the wretched prisoners were brought on their way from the cells to the scaffold. Fronting Jane Scott's chair is a window, the sill of which is formed out of the thickness of the wall. On this were placed the coffins of the condemned, in readiness for their bodies one hour from the time that they would first set eyes upon them.

Jane Scott's Chair

Lancaster Castle remained as a prison until 8th February 2012.

When closure was announced 30 Members of Parliament signed an Early Day Motion regretting the decision and pointing out that the prison ranked second in national statistics for the resettlement of offenders, which in turn had a significant impact on the crime rate in North East England.

Acknowledgements

We'd like to thank Bernard Wilson for his excellent foreword and Mick Purvis for his insight into life as a Prison Officer at HMP Lancaster.

For the author Isaac Smith in recording his experiences in the late 19th Century and of course to Auntie Eleanor who saved the booklet until a curious John found it and thought it would be great to republish it one day.

Index

OTHER BOOKS BY JOHN NIXON

All the books are available on Amazon

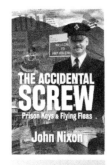

The Accidental Screw

The History of RAF Millom

Wings Over Sands

Warbirds of Walney

History of RAF Millom (Hardback)

Veterans Voices

History of RAF Millom (paperback)

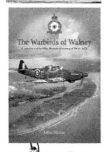

www.johnnixonauthor.co.uk

Printed in Great Britain
by Amazon

45985541R00071